LEADING LIVES

Irish Women in Britain

Rita Wall

Attic Press
Dublin

First published in Ireland in 1991 by
Attic Press
44 East Essex Street
Dublin 2

British Library Cataloguing in Publication Data
Wall, Rita
    Leading lives : Irish women in Britain.
    1. Great Britain. Women. Social conditions
    I. Title
    305.89162041

    ISBN 1-85594-020-5

Cover Design: Luly Mason
Origination: Attic Press
Printing: The Guernsey Press Co Ltd

*In celebration
of the many talents
of all Irish women,
past and present,
here and abroad*

ACKNOWLEDGEMENTS

I would like to thank the nine women who agreed to be interviewed by me for this book. Their encouragement and enthusiasm were the real incentive that kept me going.

I am indebted to Brid Boland of the London Irish Women's Centre and Ena Murtagh for their help at the initial stage in drawing up a list of possible interviewees in Britain. A special thanks to Liz Curtis for her accurate typing and helpful suggestions and to Annette Gartland for her moral support and editorial advice. I am grateful to Brid Loughran for her help in the research of female Irish stereotypes in Britain.

This book would never have happened without the support of my mother and father, Venna and Paddy, who provided me with board and lodgings and much more, while I wrote up the final drafts of the interviews. Their unceasing kindness and hospitality provided the essential backdrop so that I could cope with the minor crises and problems that tend to occur during book publication.

I would also like to publicly thank friends in Britain and Ireland, women and men, who have encouraged and supported me through the periods of doubt and frustration during the isolated times of editing and writing, particularly all those at Elizabeth House in Earls Court; Margaret Finley and Larry Brownan.

Rita Wall, May 1991

Contents

Introduction

IRISH WOMEN have made up the largest female migrant workforce in Britain for the last 100 years. In the early part of the century they worked in unskilled jobs, as nannies and maids and during the war years, as cheap factory labour. In the 1940s British hospitals welcomed a huge influx of Irish women to nursing. It is no coincidence that Irish Oscar winning actress Brenda Fricker played Megan, a formidable Irish nurse, in the popular BBC series *Casualty*. Later, and especially in the 1970s, the emigration of educated middle class Irish women became a new trend. The Irish educational system is respected and Irish graduates were a welcome commodity.

With increased IRA activity in Britain in the early 1970s and the introduction of the Prevention of Terrorism Act there was fear among the Irish population in Britain. Irish clubs abounded, and solidarity was provided there but in mainstream society many Irish people disguised their accents for fear they would be insulted, arrested or hassled. This new wave of anti-Irish prejudice played into the old stereotype of the 'thick Paddy' — an image of Irish people used by British colonialist powers throughout history. The stereotype always distances people from the individual, race or idea, and it worked very well. Irish people were seen as lesser mortals in British society.

There are several stereotypes of Irish women in Britain. There is the mystical *Mother Ireland* — a quiet, gentle, caring figure. A woman who is beautiful in an 'other worldly' sense, conjuring up images of a green and magical land across the sea. She never takes the centre of the stage but fades away into the mists when approached or confronted. This Mother Ireland is certainly not a powerful woman who demands attention, respect and her rights.

There is the stereotype of the *Irish mother*: struggling with eleven children, she is uneducated, Catholic, poor, married to an alcoholic labourer. It is a cruel image. Unsightly, not really accepted or integrated into mainstream British life, she is barely 'tolerated.'

The nun looms large in the British psyche as an eccentric view of Irish womanhood. Larger than life, she's a bible-thumping, mysterious, celibate figure, swathed in black, powerful in her own domain of school, hospital or nursing home but subservient to a male hierarchical church. She is looked upon with interest, curiosity and mild amusement.

Being a woman of any ethnic origin in Britain creates particular obstacles to rightfully claiming power in society, and persistent stereotypes are a heavy part of the burden they must carry. Britain is still a male-dominated society. Women still earn less and are more poverty stricken than men. Expectations for women are changing but top jobs in industry, health care, and education belong to men.

Institutional prejudice, physical violence, and heavy work loads, all hold women back. It is women for the most part who have been sexually abused when they were children and warned to keep quiet about it, told they are in fact to blame for it. Young women are often subjected to severe criticism from their mothers, who are preparing them for conformity to a male culture. The heavy responsibility of child rearing and housework falls for the most part on females, as children and women.

These experiences do nothing to support a woman in the world. They contribute directly to women's invisibility. Confidence is shattered, energy is low and society has not in the past opened miraculous doors to the higher echelons of power for women.

Irish women in Britain come from a Catholic culture which has traditionally placed a strong emphasis on women staying in the home. With a church ban on contraceptives, Irish women have borne the burden of large families. Though working outside the home was disapproved of, many Irish women living in Britain took menial, low-paid jobs in the struggle to make ends meet.

There is still a huge silent class barrier for many Irish women seeking work outside the home. While access to education has facilitated this move, working class Irish women are held back by a middle class society which only opens the doors of institutional power to its own. Irish working class women still have limited choices for life chances. To some extent, while middle class Irish women are now gaining entry into the ranks of British society little or nothing has changed for working class Irish women. But it is working class Irish women who have supported and serviced middle class society in Britain for years. It is they who have worked in the factories, nannied, cleaned and cooked in homes and institutions. Their work provides for the society, in a crucial material sense. But it is work for which there is no visible reward, no recognition. They remain an exploited working population, with poorer health, shorter life-spans, scant pay and no prestige. British society, like Irish society, has totally failed to acknowledge that Irish working class women are one of its most vital resources.

The winds of change are stirring. A wave of Irish pride has swept Britain in the last few years with the introduction of Irish Studies into the school curriculum, the establishment of Irish newspapers in Britain, the London-Irish Women's Centre and all kinds of consiousness-raising exercises by many Irish groups throughout Britain. Irish people are standing up in Britain, determined to challenge the stereotypes which hold them down. The release of innocent, wrongfully imprisoned Irish people following long years of intense lobbying and protest has undoubtedly enabled Irish people in Britain to develop a sense of solidarity and strength.

In this book I wanted to challenge the persistent stereotyping of Irish women. The women interviewed are all visible in Britain, each in her own field — outstanding writers, campaigners, entrepreneurs, professionals. Each one of the women interviewed has stepped out on to new ground with courage and conviction in her own ability. I have deliberately chosen to allow the women speak for themselves. Too often, women's talk is not heard or appreciated. The interviews have been edited in collaboration with the women.

Today women are beginning to make different choices. All the women interviewed in this book are pushing barriers aside, moving ahead in their goals and challenging prejudice. They are an inspiration to the new Irish arriving in Britain who see their sister country women take a central part in a different society. And it is an inspiration for those at home, to know that their Irish sisters have made themselves heard in their new destination.

There is a sadness too, that Ireland has lost these fine women. The majority of Irish women in the past have fled to England for economic reasons. But in latter years, the anti-female bias in Ireland's institutions has pushed women away and towards a space where they can be free to control their own fertility, to own their sexuality and avail of wider opportunities and resources. They have also emigrated to a new country 'for themselves' , for excitement, change and challenge. They have left Ireland to live in Britain where they believe they will be allowed to explore and celebrate their talents without prejudice.

The interviews which follow are a contribution to the slowly emerging history of Irish women in Britain. The women I spoke to, talked about many aspects of their lives and experience, traditionally censored or controlled by a male power structure. They tell us what it was like to grow up in Ireland, who their early role models were, the people who encouraged them to achieve their dreams. And they tell us, too, of their experience of emigration. They talk about spirituality, Northern Ireland, fertility, family, and relationships. They speak honestly of themselves.

For these women, their talent, intelligence and perseverance has been publicly recognised. It is important for us to celebrate that and to appreciate their strength while pushing for the same chances, encouragement and opportunities for all Irish women at home and throughout the world.

Rita Wall

Photograph: Max Whitaker

Annie Maguire

Annie Maguire was born fifty-four years ago in Belfast. She worked as a tailoress making army uniforms, as a weaver and serving tea at the Royal Victoria Hospital before emigrating to England in 1957.

In 1976 Annie Maguire, Patrick her husband, two of her children Vincent (sixteen), and Patrick (thirteen), her brother Seán Smyth, her husband's brother-in-law Giuseppe Conlon and a family friend Patrick O'Neill were charged with possessing explosives and running an IRA bomb factory and received jail sentences of between four to fourteen years.

Annie served ten years in prison, seven as a high security Category A prisoner and was the last of her family to emerge in 1985. In October 1989, when the convictions of the Guildford Four were quashed, for alleged bombing of pubs in Guildford and Woolwich, it was a follow-on legal step to establish the innocence of the 'Maguire Seven.' The seven had been arrested on the basis of discredited confessions extracted by the Surrey police from two of the Guildford Four.

In the summer of 1990, the Director of Public Prosecutions admitted that the convictions were 'unsafe and unsatisfactory.' The Home Secretary told the House of Commons that the convictions could not be allowed to stand.

The sole evidence against the Maguires— despite the strong claim made that they ran a bomb factory at their North London home — was a scientific test showing traces of nitroglycerine on their hands and on Annie's rubber gloves. She has always maintained that the only packet of rubber gloves in her house was underneath her sink, unopened.

The Inquiry into the Guildford Four and the Maguires by Sir

John May in 1990 established their innocence. The scientific test used in their presentation was found not to be 'specific' for nitroglycerine as alleged at the Maguire trial. An officer who performed the incriminating handswabs for their prosecution had been in contact with explosives prior to the Maguire arrests. No control tests were carried out on him, the Inquiry heard.

The Director of Public Prosecutions is prepared to admit that the Maguires might have been 'innocently contaminated' - but this is not good enough for Annie. It still leaves a shadow of doubt hanging over her family.

I met Annie Maguire at her North London maisonette. She was tired; the last step in her fight to clear her family's name was just around the corner and the waiting was hard. During our interview, she was advised by her solicitor not to talk in detail about her prison experience because of her case coming before the Court of Appeal in May 1991.

Since her release from prison, Annie has campaigned ceaselessly for the release of the Guildford Four and on the innocence of the Maguire Seven. She has spoken to public meetings in Ireland and England and has been interviewed extensively by the media. Annie has represented her family to government officials, church hierarchy and leading members of the British establishment.

Annie Maguire defines herself as a mother. She has four children and three grandchildren. She loves young people and works part-time as a dinner lady in a local school. She plays bingo at least once a week. If she won the pools she would like to buy a big house and care for abused children. She would also love to run a guesthouse.

ANNIE MAGUIRE

MY MAIN AIM at the moment is to get our family name cleared and to get a better life for the kids. I have four children, three sons and one daughter. I wanted to achieve for them, when they were growing up. Like other mothers I just went out and worked. It was all for them. I tried to save money in the bank for a rainy day or for their education. I was always very determined. If I set out to do something I will do it. I don't care how many knocks I get. I'll stand up again.

I was brought up in Belfast off the Grosvenor Road, the Falls area. There were five brothers, though one died when he was a baby, and three sisters. I'm the second eldest of the family. My mum's parents had a small farm. They lived in the White Rock, off the Falls. My grandmother did everything to make money. She baked soda bread and did fish and chips. She had a tea house in her home and sold chickens, eggs, and turkeys at Christmas. We had to go and sell the bread when we finished school. We'd sleep there at weekends and would have to take a basket out with a white linen cloth and deliver to the customers. I would come back and tell her that the tinkers took some, but that was a white lie. I felt sorry for the kids and gave them some.

I had a happy upbringing. I picked up from Mummy and Daddy to be honest, and never to do any wrong to people. My mother would never say one thing and then do another and that's me. I'll say what I have to say though I am not hurtful to people. I get my determination from my grandmother and mother. I know if I'm right, nobody's going to tell me I'm wrong. In 1974 when I thought the nation was against me, I still said the day

17

would come when I would prove that the decision to charge and imprison me was wrong and I was right about that.

When I was growing up I was looked upon more as a boy than as a girl. I was a bit of a tomboy. I'd climb trees quicker than any of the boys. Grandmother Clark didn't look on me as a girl or a boy it made no difference to her. 'If a man could do it, you could do it,' she'd say. She'd have given you a shovel and told you to go and clean out the hen-shed. She used to say 'Whenever you have two hands you'll never want. Never depend on anybody. Get out and do it yourself.' That's been in me since I was a kid.

There wasn't much money around, although in one sense we were luckier than other kids because, with my grandmother, we got fresh eggs. We didn't starve. My mother was also a great worker. Mummy used to sit and sew at the machine for hours, making things. She used to make mats for the bedroom floor out of nylon stockings. She showed us how to do all that and she was a great knitter. She had it really tough. She sacrificed a lot of things for herself to give to us. Mummy never went out drinking, she never wore makeup and she never spent money on clothes for herself.

She was always tidy in her cross-over apron with no sleeves, and a blouse and skirt underneath. She had one good set of clothes to go out in. When she did dress up, she looked lovely. My daddy and she were good dancers; they used to lead off in the dance hall. Her dancing days lasted until I was about five years old and then as the other kids started coming, she devoted herself to us and that's exactly what I've done to mine. I know I'm intending to live the same life as Mummy.

There used to be other people living around me in London and they seemed to have more than we did. I used to think to myself, well, their husbands probably earn better money. No matter how much I worked, the money seemed to go. Then when I used to look at my kids and people used to admire them for the way they were dressed, I used to think inside, talking to my mother, 'Well Mummy you were never one for fancy dresses or makeup and you were happy doing what I'm doing.' I'm determined, but there are times I feel I just can't be bothered and then I'll say 'You're going to be bothered.' This is Mummy in me.

The first school I went to was St Vincent's, run by nuns. I was only there for one morning. I'd seen this nun pick up this butter clopper and she banged it on the table. When I heard it, I was up and out that door, down through the Dunville Street park, home to my mummy. 'I don't want to stay at that school. It's horrible and she beats us with butter cloppers,' I said. Mummy was really very understanding and she said 'Alright we'll get you into Leeson Street,' because my sister was there. I was there from when I was five until I was eleven, and then I crossed over to St Peter's which was a bigger school. I remember in St Peter's they showed you how to set up the altar and all the bits and pieces that went on it. I used to love doing that. When you were bigger you were picked to make the teacher's coffee, milky coffee, and I remember making an extra drop and putting it into another cup for myself. At that time coffee was precious.

My father was quiet. He liked a drink but he'd always see to us first. He used to make us laugh. He collected the Pools and I remember one day he won £100. I can still see him turning the corner of Abyssinia Street with his mate, Uncle Terry. He had this big doll under one arm and a doll's house under the other. I remember him coming in saying he had won the Pools and counting out the money left over and giving it to Mummy. I asked where was the doll going to sleep. She said 'We'll make a nice cot for her,' and she cleared out the bottom of a chest of drawers and she put the doll in. 'When you were a little baby that was your cot too,' she said.

* * *

I would have loved to have gone to Orange's Secretarial Academy. Miss Orange was our head teacher and she used to say to me 'You know you've got it in you and you must use it.' But I knew that I had to leave school. I was the second eldest and Mummy needed the money. She needed our wages coming in. I remember saying to her 'I don't want to leave school,' and she said 'But you have to; we can't afford to do anything. Sure you'll start dressmaking or something like that and you'll be able to make lots of money. And you'll have your own nice dresses.' I accepted it; you had to. But I really enjoyed both schools. I never had any problems with any of the teachers.

The first job I had was in a 'stitching' room, down in the Grosvenor, making army tunics. I was a tailoress. There were four of us from the same Street started together. We were fourteen. There was a doddery old woman, Miss Gibson; she was in her mid-fifties. And the boss's name was Rogers; we nicknamed him Roy Rogers.

Miss Gibson was just short of a whip to make us work harder. I'd never been in trouble at school but I thought 'I'm not taking it. Is this what adults have to put up with?' I came home and said to Mummy 'I'm not taking this.' She says 'Give yourself time, it'll come to you.' And I said 'No, I don't want to stay.' Shortly afterwards, Miss Gibson just went too far and the boss Rogers came along and said 'Get on with your work.' I turned and said, 'Roy Rogers you can keep your job because I'm going home,' and the other three walked out with me.

When I told Mummy, she said 'Well you know I need the money. You may not get another job so easy,' but a neighbour brought us up to the Weaving shop in the Springfield the following morning, and we started.

When all the factory whistles went at six o'clock, the gates opened and we'd all run down the Springfield to the Falls. You got home and had a quick wash, had your tea and away up to the park to play your camogie. It would be about eight-thirty, nearly nine, in the evening when we'd finish the game. Then we'd come down the street, straight into the picture house, to meet Paddy and his mates.

I'd been going with him since I was fourteen. We went to the same school. He was three years older than me and when he left school he joined the British army. I remember he was in Cyprus (it was just like it is here today in England to have somebody in Belfast). It was just like it is today for soldiers in Belfast. I remember his mother sitting listening to the radio, worried when she'd hear about a British soldier being killed out there.

When we courted it wasn't like today. There was no sex in it. In fact when we got married I was still a virgin; it was the fashion then. I remember when Paddy was in Cyprus, one of my friends, Kathleen Rowan, was going out with this boy called Billy. He had a friend called Joe and his father owned a business. We all went out together a few times. Mummy said 'That's it, my girl. You get the one with the money because I don't want you struggling through life, as I've struggled.' But I said that Paddy Maguire was my boyfriend and I wouldn't give him up. I had a strong feeling about Paddy. It just didn't happen with anyone else. He wasn't a loud mouth and he wasn't a pusher either. He showed respect for me. He didn't try anything on me and that's a thing I recognised and felt was important.

I remember one night sitting in the picture house when Paddy was away, and this fellah came in and put his arm round me. I said 'Do you mind, you don't do that to me.' He said 'Oh, you're no different than anyone else,' and I said 'I am.' He touched me. I got up in the middle of the picture house and I gave him a wallop. A couple of Paddy's mates heard the commotion and said 'What's the matter?' I said 'It's alright. I've dealt with it.' The fellah just got up and walked out. He came back to me months later and he shook my hand and said 'I'm sorry.' I said 'Nobody does that to me.'

When we got engaged, Paddy thought that it was the first step before marriage and he could have his way. I took the ring off and opened our front door and flung it out. I said 'If you think a ring can make me do things that I don't want to do, you're mistaken. You take your ring and go.'

I was downstairs, sobbing my heart out and my mummy came down. She made me cocoa and says 'Come on, tell me what happened.' I said 'Nothing,' and she says 'Come on, tell me what happened; he didn't bang that door for nothing,' so I told her. She said 'They all try it. He'll be back tomorrow and he'll think the world of you. If you had given in, you would never have got a second ring on your finger.' And lo and behold he came round the next morning. I said 'I don't want to see you,' and he said 'Alright but how about going out to the pictures?' So we just made up, and when we were getting married and sex came up again, he said to me 'If you had given in to me, there's no way I'd have come back.'

* * *

We got married on 26 September 1957 and that night we sailed for England. I came here on the understanding that it would be only for a year or two, to save up enough money to go back and buy a house in Belfast. I'm here now thirty-three years.

I remember being disappointed with our first bedsit so I was determined to get something better. I went after an ad for accommodation. It was a house near us. A woman, Mrs Lupin, opened the door and I asked her had she a room. She asked me had I any children. I said 'No, we've just got married.' She said 'Are you Irish?' I said 'Yes, I'm from Belfast.' She said 'Belfast?' I said 'Northern Ireland.' 'You speak differently to the other Irish around here,' she said. I was invited in and when we started talking it was like I had known her all my life. She said later on that she felt the same about me. She showed me the basement. It was a bedsit, but it looked better than the other one because of the garden at the back and it had an open fire. She became like a second mother to me. She called me 'Annie' and ever since then that has stuck.

When I missed a period I was worried sick. I was thinking I had cancer or something. Mrs Lupin asked me was there anything wrong. When I told her she laughed. I asked her 'What's so funny? Aren't you supposed to have them every month?' She said 'Don't you think you're having a baby?' I was shocked. 'It's natural, love, when you're married,' she said. I said 'I didn't know. Mummy didn't tell me anything. We were just told not to let the boys touch you.' Mrs Lupin took me to the doctor. I was pregnant. I couldn't wait to tell Paddy when he came home in the evening. He says 'I had an idea you were.' He knew but I didn't.

Even though Mrs Lupin's was cosier I was still 'going home' every weekend. Paddy used to say 'There's a big boat and a big plane that goes every evening. You go but I'm not going with you.' I used to cry and phone Mummy up. I used to phone the pub on the corner and they would call down the Street, 'Annie's on the phone.' Mummy would come running up. She'd tell me 'You've made your bed now, you must lie in it.'

I got a job in a nursery, and as Vincent's birth got nearer, people were very nice to me. I always got on well with English people. I almost died having Vincent — it was a caesarian birth.

When he was born I had something to occupy myself with. I was a mother. Paddy was happier and I was sensible enough to know that if I had forced him to go back to Belfast, it probably wouldn't have worked out. He would have come back here again and that's no marriage, no place for a child when two parents are separated, one working away and coming back occasionally. Eleven months later John came. I'd plenty to keep me going.

* * *

When times are hard I always fall back on my faith in God. I believe there is something there; there's got to be. God makes heaven and hell on earth. If bad things happen to you here on earth, that is hell. When you actually do die, you're not going to suffer anymore. If people go out to deliberately hurt you, I have this feeling that they're the devil's people, the devil working in people.

When I was in prison, I remember I could not take any more; this was near the beginning of my sentence. Not having the children, I was stopped in my tracks of being a mother, and that was my life. I was really crying after a visit from Anne-Marie, my daughter. I was desperate. I was saying 'I don't want to live, I just don't want to live.' And this voice in my head said 'Stop that kind of talk. Get up and get on with it.' I sat up and looked at a Sacred Heart picture and said 'Right, God, it's you and me against the nation. You're bringing me through this.' I told the girls in the wing and they laughed but I never turned back.

When you die I believe your soul goes wherever it's got to go and I believe that there is another world. I suppose it's all fruits and trees. That's how I picture it anyway. I hope it is because I'm looking forward to it.

I am a Catholic. When I was growing up if you mentioned to the priest that you had a boyfriend, he would advise you to break up the relationship. When I was married, the priest forbade any use of contraception. I remember after Patrick, I knew I didn't want another child until I had him reared. I went to confession and the priest asked 'How many children have you, and their ages?' I told him, three. Patrick the youngest was now three years old. 'What have you been doing for the last three years? The first

23

two were very quick; there's a three year gap now. Are you using anything?' I said 'No,' and he asked 'Is your husband?' I said 'No.' 'Are you having full sex?' he asked, and I said 'Yes.' He said 'I can't understand this. You should have had another three children.' 'Father,' I said, 'I couldn't cope.' He said 'Nonsense, you can cope. God doesn't send them out into the world unless he knows they're going to be fed.' I said to him, 'That may be so, Father, but here in London I can just about feed the three I have. Would you come and put a loaf of bread on my table if I get pregnant because I'll have to stop work and there'll be very little money coming in?' He didn't give me absolution or a blessing, and I felt very hurt but he didn't stop me believing in my faith.

* * *

I was thirty-nine when I was lifted by the police. It happened in 1974. I had a big house and would have owned it today as the council had just informed us that we could buy our own houses. I'd have got it for £14,000. My aunt and uncle in Kennington were going to get me the mortgage on their house to buy it. I lost out on that because of prison.

I was doing four part-time jobs at that time. Paddy had been out of work for a couple of months. Vincent was just about to leave school and John would have been free the following year, so that would have been more money coming in.

Paddy (my brother), Giuseppe (my brother-in-law) and Pat O'Neill (a friend), had gone to the pub to have a drink before they went home. Pat had left his kids with me as his wife was having her fourth baby. I was out putting on the washing machine. They *(the police)* knocked at the door. Anne-Marie answered it and they sent her flying.

I could see these men through the window. It was a long hall but I'd seen their shapes and thought it was Paddy and the others back. They said 'Mrs Maguire, Anne Maguire?' I said 'That's me and who are you?' They told me to turn off the machine and come into the sitting room. I went in and the dogs were in the hallway and I wouldn't pass them because I was frightened of big dogs. They moved them. They asked about Gerard Conlon and I said I didn't know anything about Gerard Conlon. I said I knew more about the young boy who lives next door than I do about Gerard Conlon or indeed any of my nephews or nieces in Ireland. They live over there. I live here. I told them that Gerard Conlon's father had arrived in London. Giuseppe Conlon was Paddy's brother-in-law, and Gerard's father. They weren't satisfied with the answers and they said we had to go down to the police station.

They went off and arrested the men in the pub and they took me and the three boys to the police station. I left Anne-Marie and the three O'Neill kids in my big bed and I gave them a kiss. I told Anne-Marie, who had started to tremble, not to cry. I told her I wouldn't be long. 'I'm going to help the police and I'll be back,' I said. She put her arms around me and I kissed her; the same with the other kids. The next time I saw her it was five months later. They just put us away.

They took us to Guildford the next morning for interrogation. I was beaten up and pushed around. I couldn't believe that these were police officers who we'd brought our children up to respect. I knew that I'd never been on the wrong side of the law and I had done no wrong. If this was how they were treating me, an innocent person, how did they treat actual criminals?

I had my period and they made me stand spread-eagled against the wall, and every time I fell with weakness, they kicked me to get back up again. I hadn't changed my sanitary towel. There was just one little officer slipped me a towel and said 'Give me the dirty one.' And I said I couldn't give it to anyone. 'Mrs Maguire,' she said, 'please throw it into this bag,' and that was the only one I got. I was there seven days.

They asked me questions and put a gun to my head. I don't suppose it was loaded but I didn't know that. They hit me about the head and pulled my hair back, putting a light in my eyes. My eyes were sore as I didn't have my glasses. They called me names, saying that I wasn't a mother, I was 'a prostitute.' They said I wasn't fit to have my children back and they were going to get the worst foster parents they could find in England and send my Patrick and Anne-Marie to them. I was crying inwardly; tears weren't coming. They were calling me a hard Irish bitch because I wasn't crying. Shock, it must have been shock, because I cry if anybody hurts other people. I was pinching myself to see if I was alive or dreaming. One young officer gave me a kick in the hip as I left the interrogating room. I just flew down the corridor and into a room at the bottom of it. I landed right on top of a bed. I remember another young officer's face looking at me as much as to say 'I can't help you and I don't agree with this.' The first one turned around and said 'Look at the Irish bastard and she doesn't even cry.'

The females officers were worse than the men. I remember thinking 'If you could do this to me, what could you do to your own mother?' That officer was only a kid but I suppose because of the Guildford bombs they were angry and to them we were Irish terrorists.

They charged us with murder first and I just remember screaming out. I couldn't cry. I just kept screaming 'No I'm not guilty. I'm not guilty of murdering any child. I love children. I love everybody, and I'm not guilty.' They took us in a van to Brixton. They opened the door and two young officers were waiting for us. I remember them coming forward and me backing away, screaming 'Please don't hit me, don't hit me anymore.' Those officers talked about it for days. One, Cara was her name, became a good friend. They couldn't believe the state that I was in. She came over and said 'Love, we're not going to hit you. We don't hit anybody. We want to help you.'

I would like to see Ireland free but I do not agree with violence and would never get involved in any terrorist organisation. No way at all. I have always had too much to mind with my family. I do not believe that violence achieves anything.

It has been said that Gerard's confession of our names was taken under duress. I remember when Gerard was born. I was a teenager and I used to visit him. I was very fond of him. At his first birthday I had a photographer up getting photos taken in his grandfather's house. His grandfather was dying and I had photos taken of Gerard with his grand-da. It's just hard to understand. Where did he get the right to use my name in his statement? Gerard has rung me once since he came out and said that it was Paul Hill who mentioned my name first. I don't know who to believe. Three families, because of naming of names, were destroyed. My children were left orphans for ten years. They were stripped of everything. We were innocent people.

I was interrogated. And as a mother and a woman I stood up to the beatings because I knew the truth. Look at the Birmingham Six. Look at the beatings those men took. Did they mention any innocent names? No; they knew the truth.

Maybe they felt because we were never involved in anything, that we would never have been taken in. For whatever reason it backfired, because Gerard's own father had arrived at our house, and was arrested, charged and died in prison. It hurt me more when Giuseppe died in prison because it was my name that Gerard had mentioned. If my name had never come up, his father would not have died in that prison cell.

I went on hunger strike for three weeks because of Giuseppe. I wanted to see him before he died. He was very ill in prison and I just wanted to do something to show people that we were innocent. I received a message from Paddy, my husband. He said if I didn't come off the hunger strike he was going on one, and he would never come off it. I knew he meant it. I knew that if I weakened, Paddy would weaken, Vincent would weaken and Patrick would weaken. I couldn't harm them. So I stopped. One of the prison warders, Joanie Barr, talked sense into me.

If you respected the prison warders they would respect you. There were some kind wardens. They were homely women doing a job to feed their families. We had fun with them. At night when they would close the bedroom doors, they'd whisper 'Have you got everything ready for beddy bye byes now?' There were a few younger ones who, when they had their uniforms on, let the power go to their heads. But you just laughed that off and made sure if one of them was getting at you, that you had another inmate around to witness any misbehaviour on their part.

Being in prison with so many women was like all hell broke loose. There were so many people in there for all sorts of different crimes. Many of the prisoners did not get on with each other and it was very tense.

My sister Mary McCaffery and her husband Hugh really supported us through our horror. They took two of my children to Belfast and raised them as their own. If I ever wrote a depressing letter from the prison, Mary would often send a bouquet of flowers to cheer me up. Along with my aunt and uncle, the Kearneys in Kennington, they kept our spirits up and no matter what reports were published, stood by us. When you have people who believe in you, you can carry on.

After ten years, when I was released, I knew that I had lost my children. When I came out the boys were men and Anne-Marie was a young woman. I had to get to know them again. They were different people.

* * *

My children were born here and I will stay with them in Britain. I know that as a mother. My strength comes from my children. I always try to listen to them and stick with them through thick and thin. I get on with all nationalities in London, including English people. I have forgiven those who have wronged me and my family. (I get that from my mother.) I feel pity for those who go out to harm others; they probably have had something terrible done to them in their lives. If you don't forgive and you hold bitterness and hate in your heart, you will be the only one to suffer. Let it go. Let the hatred go and ask God to forgive those who hurt you.

England is not good for women on their own. It's dangerous. You can't walk around even to do your shopping; there are too many muggings. I wouldn't advise an Irish person who has a job at home to come here to live. You are better off staying with your own people.

Personal truths

Always be honest with yourself and with others. It does pay.

Never depend on others. If you really want something in life, you should go all out to get it.

If you've got determination you will be a success.

Photograph: AP/RN

Eileen Pollock

Born in Belfast, Eileen Pollock or 'Polly' to friends, is forty-three. She was educated by Dominican nuns and at Queen's University Belfast where she graduated with a BA in languages. She emigrated to England in 1969 to train as a technical translator.

*Her first love for the theatre had been kindled during her university days and her career in this field started as an assistant stage manager at the **Bush Theatre** in Hammersmith, London. From behind the scenes she took the step to appear on stage and shortly afterwards joined a socialist Theatre Company called **Belt and Braces** for a five year stint.*

*Always pursuing her own writing and work she moved on to co-found two theatre companies in succession, **Bloomers** and **Camouflage**. She has worked with Ireland's **Field Day Company** and the **Druid Theatre Company** and with various English repertory and touring companies.*

*She is currently playing the Dublin 'tart', Lilo Lil, in the popular sitcom **Bread** for BBC. When I interviewed her she was just finishing the West End run of a theatre production of **Bread**. From the West End she was booked for a play at the Lyric in Belfast which will be followed by a new series of **Bread**. She is also working on a new project in collaboration with a painter, musician and writer which she hopes will tour international venues in the summer.*

I interviewed Eileen at her London base in Whitechapel. She also has a home in Galway on the west coast of Ireland where she loves to rest and 'breathe.' She would like to star in a major film in the future and is always on the look-out for new and challenging roles. She also has an ardent ambition to explore her own writing even further.

A breathless speaker, Eileen is a vivacious raconteur. She talks with her hands, eyes and facial expressions. She draws on a depth of experience and sincere thoughtfulness. She exudes a childlike zest and enthusiasm for life which is infectious.

Photograph: Joe Geoghegan

EILEEN POLLOCK

AT THIS VERY MOMENT I'm working on *Bread*, a stage version of the television sitcom, written by Carla Lane. I play Lilo Lil, who is referred to as 'the tart' because she is the girlfriend of the father of the Liverpool family who are the main characters. Whenever people recognise me in a supermarket they say things like, 'I don't want to be rude, but I'm afraid you remind me of the tart in *Bread*,' and I say, 'Well, I play the part, so you're not being rude but she's not a tart; it's the father of the family who is.'

Lilo Lil was supposed to be Liverpudlian, and I couldn't do the accent for long enough to be convincing. I tried for a bit with the help of a local youth group. I practised it on a cab driver and he asked me what part of Australia I came from. So when I went for the audition I said, 'Do you think she could actually come from Ireland — like be an Irish woman, not first generation, just from Ireland?' They thought that was OK. They liked it.

Lilo Lil is a stereotype in comedy. She is a woman who doesn't conform, 'the tart,' not the wife. She's supposed to be more exciting. She's got bigger breasts, higher heels, more make-up. She's wilder in bed. Men love that idea. But they would never bring her home.

Some of the feminist press won't interview me now because they think I've sold out, playing such a stereotype. I feel sad about that. Not that I feel spurned, but I feel that the idea hasn't been taken on board. I'd rather they would interview me and say 'Defend yourself!' And I will.

The feminist movement is very wide and as far as I'm concerned includes 'tarts' and prostitutes. Lilo Lil is not a prostitute, but if she was I would defend her right to be a prostitute given the probable economic circumstances involved. I don't appreciate the fact that a woman has to sell her body, but then (big statement here!), marriage might be construed in some cases as the same thing. If the situation is set up that women's bodies are to be had, to be used, to be paid for housekeeping or money, then why not use them? Until women's bodies are no longer seen, even by themselves, as objects to be had and used, morality doesn't come into it.

When I was a child, I used to write poems. I was on BBC Radio Children's Hour in Belfast reading my work when I was seven. At eleven, I wrote a nativity play. My sister was Joseph. She was awful. She stood in front of the baby Jesus. My neighbour was Mary because she was beautiful. And three girls, who I swore I would never speak to again, were the shepherds and the angel.

This angel went and appeared to the shepherds. She got her speeches wrong, and told them they were about to conceive in their wombs and bring forth a son and his name was to be Jesus. And the two wee shepherds were, you know, in giggles. It was awful. It was in my granny's drawing room. Some of the boys from the next street were in. I fancied one of them, so I was mortified.

When I went to grammar school that all fell away. I presume I went to the theatre because I think my mother was interested. She would take us to the theatre at the Lyric, the Circle and the Group in Belfast. But she was not encouraging as far as a career in theatre was concerned. My mother wanted me to be a teacher or a nurse. My father wanted me to be a civil engineer, but he told me too late and I had the completely wrong subjects for it.

* * *

I have one sister. My father and mother both worked when we were young. Sometimes when we came home from school there was nobody in the house so we would let ourselves in. We were the notorious latch-key kids. It didn't harm us one bit. We got Daddy's tea ready — when we remembered. Once we didn't and the cry went up 'Three big women in the house and no tea.' My mother would come in about ten or eleven at night from work in my grandfather's shop. She would immediately get stuck in doing the dishes with her coat on. We told her we'd do it when we'd finished our homework. She carried on. I often find myself doing exactly the same thing now.

I had two main role models when I was growing up. One was my granny. You know how you never class your mother as important. Your mother's your mother. So forget about your mother; you always forget her. My granny was wonderful. She was 'Our Nana.'

When I was at school I would say to my friends 'Come along, I'm going to my granny's to spend the evening there after school.' They would say 'But I don't know how to talk to old women.' They needn't have bothered. She would regale them with stories and songs. She was from Tyrone and her grandfather was a native Irish speaker. She had the gold *fáinne* herself.

They came to Belfast when she was seven. In her lifetime she stood in awe at the first horseless carriage that went up the Falls Road. It was a tram and 'the devil's work.' Then fifty years on, she was flying to America to see her daughter and her grandchildren. She had a lot to say. She was fascinating. Big, fat, but not loud. She made me feel important. She played Big Ears to my Noddy in her bedroom when I was five.

Nana was a proper Christian. She wasn't a Holy Joe. She used to pray for Kruschev and his wife and the Russians who she thought were deep-down lapsed Irish Catholics. I admired her. Her son, Gussie, was also a huge influence in my life. He was a non-macho man, and there weren't that many adults who taught me how to see magic in the simplest of things.

When I left school with all my A-levels except English, I was seventeen. I had a year to play around with. I was too young to go to Queen's University. So I decided to do something interesting. Rather than go back to school, I went to Spain. My parents let me go. I just went! 'Bye' and went off.

When I arrived I realised that I was a complete foreigner in a very strange place, and my A-level Spanish wasn't really that good. I was in a country where the heat sat on you. I thought when I arrived that Spain had a glass roof over it, it was so hot. I had to wait all day in Madrid for my connection to a remote town, where I was to be a companion to a sixteen year old girl. I went to the pictures to cool off. It was *South Pacific*, dubbed, and I couldn't understand why those Americans were speaking Spanish. Eventually though I found my feet.

Both at school and later at university I found out that people wanted me 'as a woman' to be a teacher. Because I was at a grammar school they didn't expect me to be a secretary; that was a subtle difference between the comprehensive and the grammar school. But as women, we weren't going to be lawyers, or musicians or actors. We were all going to be teachers.

* * *

My family are Catholic. My father was a policeman. It was very unusual for a Catholic to be in the RUC (*Royal Ulster Constabulary*). He once came fourth in the country in his police exams but had to wait fifteen years for promotion, by which time enough Catholics had died or retired. Catholics were supposed to be welcome, but there was only a small quota. My father risked alienating himself from his own community by joining the police force. But he joined up because it was better money. Three quid a week he got, instead of ten-and-six on the Bann drainage scheme, an outdoor relief job in the thirties. They let him in because he was good at football.

The war in Northern Ireland is not about Catholicism and Protestantism. It's not a religious war at all. It's a war of prestige, it's a war of place and society and identity. It's not about the way you pray to your God. I think the border should be removed in Ireland. A lot of problems continue because of that divide between the Republic of Ireland and Northern Ireland. The government in Britain continues to baulk at taking the loyalists of Northern Ireland to task and the people in the Republic of Ireland refuse to educate themselves about the divided needs of the Northern Ireland people. It's no more a religious war than Saddam Hussein's war is. Having said that, the Catholic-based laws of the Republic would need to change to accomodate progress towards uniting the communities.

I feel lucky to have escaped the Catholic religion, from

knitting things badly for the black babies. Do you know what I used to do? I used to bite my thumb to see how much pain I could withstand for when the communists would roll up the Lagan. How much pain I could stand for Jesus? Crazy. The 'Red Peril,' that's what we called it. And then there was the 'yellow Peril.' Enemies everywhere.

Being a Catholic was like being a member of a club, like the Masons. For me this 'club' did nothing for women. I wonder sometimes of all the religions which one would I choose? There's Islam; it's rotten for women. Then there are parts of the world where women have to have clitorectomies as part of their religious heritage. I'd fight against that. But I wouldn't fight on a religious basis; it would have to be on humanitarian terms.

The religions that we live with these days were not invented or created or developed by women. Nuns in the church are to me subservient to priests, tending to them and looking after them. It's not that priests are necessarily the most arrogant people in the world, but they appear to be. People elevate them to a god-given position; they're more special than us. I'm not even bitter about it now. None of it means anything to me now. I can look at it all with a cold eye and wonder why?

* * *

When I die, I think I'll go into the soil. And some people will remember me. I don't think my soul will go anywhere. If I've influenced anybody, I will carry on in terms of them carrying on. Like Gussie and Granny in me.

If you ask me if I've had what you might term 'psychic' experiences, I'd have to say maybe. In a flat when I was translating, sitting on the floor using my bed as a desk, I was tired. I looked up and there was a guy sitting in an armchair very near me. I just thought, 'Get rid of it, get rid of it,' and it disappeared. I am prepared to believe that it was an hallucination, but if somebody says it was a reconstruction of somebody who used to be there because their energy was still there, I'm also prepared to believe that. But I don't believe in heaven or hell.

Another time, I was working near Earls court and my friend

was working in South London. I thought I heard her call my name. So I phoned her at work and they told me that she'd taken the afternoon off and she was on her way home. She was very distressed. I don't know how to explain this because I'm not mystical at all, but I think that I knew she was in a bad way, and perhaps I was waiting for this call.

We've been reclaiming our spirituality, well we have gone searching for ancient symbols in the past like the Sheela-na-gigs. I love all that old wisdom. I think there were things that were known then to women which have been lost. Because we are women, and the next generation comes out of us, we are special. I think our male forefathers felt threatened at some point and stepped in. The very discipline of male religions and structures beat down our real spirituality.

When I die, my body will go into the earth. The earth, in a very short length of time in cosmic terms, will disintegrate or the sun will probably blow out. We'll become some kind of dust, and who knows, maybe we'll form another planet or star. I'll be involved in that action because there'll be a little bit of dust that used to be me out there. Then I'll really be a star shining bright. Dead a billion years before you've heard of me.

* * *

I decided to come to England in 1969 after getting a degree from Queen's University. When I was a fresher, I wanted to join the drama society, but I hadn't got the nerve. I went back the next year, when I had more confidence, joined up and loved it. When I left I was mad about theatre. I wanted to do a postgraduate course in Manchester and I was told by this awful careers adviser that 'It's not possible, if you haven't a double honours in English.' He put me down, telling me that he had a sister who had been an actress and how skilful she was. Then I thought I'd be a translator. He again put me down, telling me that he had been a translator during the war, with seven different languages ranging from Chinese to Arabic. He insisted that you had to be trilingual from birth in order to be a translator. 'Go teach,' he said. It was what we girls were always told. Teachers or nurses, both highly skilled jobs, neither of which I have any talent for. I didn't take his advice. I went to London and found a course in technical translation and became a translator.

I was very excited to come to London. I thought this is it. I was here to travel around the world as a qualified international technical translator. I started out socially in a small Irish group of ex-Queen's students. I was in London six months before I met a Londoner.

I studied technical translation in the day, and at night did drama classes. I also worked for a cleaning agency which makes my friends laugh. I am the least domesticated person you could encounter. Then at other people's dinner parties I was their 'good Irish girl.' I was a status symbol.

Though I was doing freelance translating I knew I wanted to be part of the drama world. I got a job at the Bush Theatre in Shepherd's Bush as an Assistant Stage Manager, general dogsbody. My wages were seven pounds a week. Somebody was sick and I started acting. My earnings were still about seven quid a show, gradually going up to twelve. I then got a job which had to have an equity card, and my wages leapt to eighteen quid.

A company came into the theatre, Belt 'n' Braces Roadshow, a socialist touring theatre company, and I loved what they did. I never considered myself a socialist before I saw them, but I adored their show. It was magnificent. I responded to it. Obviously I remember politics in Belfast but I don't remember thinking of any political identity there, except that I came from the Catholic side of the fence. In fact I am a socialist.

The things this theatre company were talking about and performing excited me. I knew this was what I wanted to be involved in. It didn't have to be Shakespeare — in fact I threw in a West End understudy job to join them. Though the socialism was fine, the male chauvinism eventually pushed me to leave and co-found Bloomers. We billed ourselves as a three woman comedy team. We examined humour in women's issues and their lives.

Women's humour is different from men's. Men tend to rap off their jokes, 'Here's the one about this ... and there's the one about that ... and did you hear the one about ...' It's to do with competition, being the life and soul of the party, scoring. Women do score as well but their humour is not based on one-liners. It's more the funny story. It's more anecdotal. We do live differently; we have different perceptions. Still, some men are tremendous raconteurs; they are the better male comedians.

From Bloomers, I was involved in founding another company, Camouflage, which was a mixed company though founded by women. We wanted to talk about issues which weren't deemed to be in the female arena, like warfare or Einstein or property.

I've been lucky in my theatre work and the opportunities I've had to be involved in brilliant plays. From my experience a good play usually means that as an actor you've come away knowing things you never knew before, and that you have been poorly paid!

* * *

I am heterosexual. Looking back, everybody wanted me to be a heterosexual but they didn't like me to go out with boys. I'm actually very shy. The awful thing was that you had to wait for somebody to fancy you — and if somebody fancied you, he could have three legs, two horns and a tail but if he fancied you, then you were elevated as a person, you were on a pedestal. I would sit and think, I fancy him, I fancy him, I fancy him, I wish he would ask me to dance, I wish he would ask me to dance. I would never go up and say 'Are you dancing?' Many, many years later I learned to ask and be prepared to be rebuffed. It isn't easy.

I regret never getting married because I'm the only person I know who's not been divorced. No, I don't believe in marriage. It's not good for people. I don't mean coupling isn't good for people — if people want to share their lives together, that's fine. I don't understand why you've got to have the stamp of an outside agency to say it's alright. The assumption, 'If you're married, then it'll last. If you're not, it might not,' smacks of mistrust. A lot of people ask me, 'Were you never married?' I answer that fortunately most of the men who have been my lovers are wise enough not to ask me to marry them. I do have companions.

Around where I live in London, the majority of people are

Bengali. The children often ask me, 'Are you a girl or a woman?' I'm forty-three. They can't understand the concept of a woman who hasn't got a husband or any children.

I'm sure I dreamed of boyfriends but I don't remember wedding bells and children. When I was at college, a guy I was going out with (when will we find better language to describe these things?) introduced me once as his girlfriend. I was eighteen and my hackles rose. I was in company so 'I couldn't be rude,' but I remember thinking, I'm not your girlfriend, I'm not something that belongs to you.

Maybe I never married because I remember a time when my parents didn't get on very well. I saw two people who hardly knew each other who were having to bring me and my sister up. They had other children who died at birth and they must have had hard times, but I wasn't sure then whether they liked each other or not, but they were together. At times it didn't seem like a good idea to me. They seem very fond of each other now and I'm glad they're still together but I didn't see anything to be had out of marriage.

I think the most important thing in my life is my very good network of brilliant mates. They're a gang and to me they're 'my gang.' And some of 'my gang' are men. I spend a lot of time writing letters, keeping up with all of them.

I never wanted children. I'm too selfish. I was such a horrible child myself. Stubborn. Bad-tempered. My poor mother. Of course I've turned out a delight as an adult. I have been sterilised. I wanted to do it years ago. The doctor said 'Certainly. And when did you complete you family?' I said 'The day I started menstruating.' She was horrified and initially refused. I was on the pill. I was thirty-five and didn't smoke so I wasn't a complete danger area but I didn't want to continue 'contracepting' myself and endangering my health. I've never regretted the decision. It doesn't impair your sexuality and it's easier on your health.

* * *

Certainly, living away from home makes you freer to make some decisions. But I don't think that London is the 'be-all and end-all' of life. Here in Whitechapel, we live in the shadow of high-rise finance houses and similar institutions, encroaching on us all the time. They are commanding Ireland's life as well but you notice it here. I hate London, but a dose of it is probably good for you every so often. I would prefer to live in Ireland and be mobile enough to go where the work is. I come from Belfast but Galway is my adoptive home. In a traffic jam in London the thought of it lifts my spirits and helps me survive.

I'm currently working on a new project with an artist friend called *Macedonia*, on material and personal identity. My gift for writing has not as yet been internationally recognised. Maybe with this new project ...

I love my life, and I consider myself very lucky. I feel blessed that I have two eyes to see things. Life is fascinating, miraculous and overwhelming. There are dark days but I feel either daft or fortunate in tending to err on the optimistic side.

Personal truths

Trust your friends and don't abandon them if you marry or go off with somebody.

You can't go through life on your own.

In fifty years time there won't be a word about it.

Relax, relax.

Ruth Dudley Edwards

Historian, writer and former British civil servant Ruth Dudley Edwards, now forty-six, was born in Dublin. The youngest of three children, she studied history at the National University of Ireland and at Cambridge (Girton and Wolfson Colleges). She was awarded a Doctorate of Literature for her published work and is currently working on a history of **The Economist.**

Ruth emigrated to England in 1965. Living in Cambridge, her first job was lecturing in Liberal Studies and English at a college of further education. While working in the British Post Office, she wrote **An Atlas of Irish History** *(1973), and followed this by an acclaimed biography,* **Patrick Pearse: the Triumph of Failure** *in 1977. Her biography of James Connolly in 1981 was well received while her biography of Victor Gollancz (1987) won the James Tait Black Memorial Prize.*

For relaxation, she writes crime novels and has had three published. These draw on her experience of working in Britain. The first, **Corridors of Death,** *was based on her time in the British civil service — she was a principal in the Department of Industry. It was shortlisted for the John Creasy Best First Crime Novel Award. All three form part of what will be a sequence of novels based on the British establishment. She has written many book reviews on history, current affairs and fiction for English and Irish newspapers and journals including the* **Economist,** *the* **Irish Independent,** *the* **Irish Press, The Irish Times** *and the* **Independent.**

Passionately interested in improving Anglo-Irish relations, Ruth has been Chairwoman of the British Association for Irish Studies since its foundation in 1986. The association has been successful in initiating programmes on the study of Ireland in universities and colleges, and in primary and secondary schools around Britain. The association has been instrumental in setting up an Institute of Irish Studies at Liverpool University and A-levels in Irish Studies.

Ruth has also been a member of the executive of the British-Irish Association for nearly a decade. This organisation arranges conferences for politicians and commentators from Britain and Ireland. The association's aim is to promote a greater understanding through dialogue.

An experienced speaker, she has given lectures and seminars in Ireland, Britain and the United States. She has broadcast in Britain and Ireland and has presented an hour-long television programme on Patrick Pearse.

I interviewed Ruth in her home in West London. Listing friendship as her main hobby, the house is open to a passing parade of friends from around the world and from all walks of life. Gentle and gracious, she does not crave public attention but prefers to work behind the scenes.

Married twice, she is now separated and has no children. I met her just before Christmas when she was packing her holiday bags for a trip to India with a friend.

RUTH DUDLEY EDWARDS

I WAS SENT to a primary school called Scoil Mhuire — a 'concentration camp' in Marlborough Street in Dublin. Every class had roughly fifty children, forty-five who came from the slums and five of whom were the children of intellectuals who were there because the teaching was through Irish. Few of the girls could go on to secondary education. The waste of talent appalled me even then.

My mother taught there. Up to her marriage she had been a lecturer in a teacher training college, but she had to give that up because of the marriage ban.* I was always conscious that she was constrained in her career. My father was a professor of Irish History at University College Dublin. His mother was a rabid Irish republican who was hiding guns in 1916 and tried to get him — when he was twelve years old — to join up during the Civil War on the republican side. His father was an English Methodist turned Quaker. My father loved his gentle and thoughtful father and hated his fanatical and quarrelsome mother. His peculiar upbringing made him fascinated by history and obsessed with the idea of objectivity. He took his PhD at London University and in partnership with Theo Moody — later professor of Irish history at Trinity — set out to make Irish history professional rather than propagandist.

My mother was the daughter of an illiterate though highly intelligent gamekeeper on an Anglo-Irish estate. She was a gifted linguist and better read than anyone I've ever known (except now perhaps my brother). She was a gifted scholarship child who later took a Celtic Studies degree. She had a great sympathy for

45

the Anglo-Irish and a great affection for their way of life and the tradition it represented. She was angry and sad that so many of the Anglo-Irish were effectively driven out of Ireland. It was she who gave the three of us an enduring love of English literature.

I grew up in a large Edwardian house where my grandmother lived upstairs denouncing Britain, de Valera and other 'traitors,' my father sat in the middle of the house pursuing the holy grail of objectivity, while my mother was downstairs talking books — from Shakespeare to PG Wodehouse. England for me was literature and films: I never saw her as the enemy. The propaganda at Scoil Mhuire and from my grandmother I always thought was garbage. I saw England as a friendly and familiar place — even a refuge from the repressions of Ireland.

I always hated and was profoundly bored by school. Although the Sacred Heart Convent was an improvement on Scoil Mhuire (there was no corporal punishment), I disliked the snobbery, narrowness and the Catholic ethos. I moved to Sandymount High School when I was fourteen and though it was much more civilised, my loathing of school was so ingrained that I simply couldn't bear it. My brother and sister had been to UCD and at sixteen I was a university groupie. Against family opposition, but with my father's backing, I left school eighteen months early, matriculated and went to college at just seventeen.

* * *

My grandmother was a militant feminist and my mother one in practice. My mother worked all her life and preached the virtues of economic independence. Yet I realise now that even at sixteen, I wanted a husband. My mother would have been appalled if I had admitted it, but I was typical of the girls of my generation. University was there to provide husbands as well as degrees. It was a great relief to me when I got engaged to Patrick Cosgrave at seventeen. I was able to go through college, making enduring friendships with men as well as women, throwing myself into student societies and not having to worry about marriage prospects.

Patrick was very gifted. He was one of the few working-class people I knew in UCD. His mother was industrious, selfless and stiflingly pious and nationalistic. He reacted by wanting to be British. I responded to his guts, brains and breadth. I owe him a lot. He bubbled with intellectual ideas and opinions and argued ferociously. Much of it passed above my head, but his enthusiasm was infectious. His heroes were men like Lawrence of Arabia and Churchill. His manifold interests included history, literature, British politics and the balance of power — everything except parochial Irish affairs. All this attracted me. Patrick took me out of Ireland. I could have married someone else, had a child in nine months and be living now in the back of beyond. We emigrated the day we married.

I abandoned Catholicism at sixteen. I simply didn't believe anymore. I found the religion illogical and I particularly disliked the authoritarian nature of the clergy. I'm a natural anti-cleric. Patrick had also lapsed. Both of us used to go through the charade on Sunday morning of pretending to go to mass and sitting it out in 'the local.' In fact my parents didn't mind when I told them my views on religion, but Patrick's mother would have been distraught. However, we were able to come out of the closet at university, and we did one heroic thing which in retrospect I am very proud of. We sat through the ringing of the Angelus Bell in the library and after a few days others followed suit. This was in the early sixties before the student revolution, so it was a massive gesture. In the same spirit, we used to go forth on Friday to find a restaurant serving meat and consume it somewhat ostentatiously.

At this time Catholics were banned by the archbishop of Dublin, John Charles McQuaid, from going to Trinity, which was seen as a danger to faith and morals. Through the Inter-university History Students' Association (founded by my father) and the debating competitions in which Patrick took part, we associated with Protestant contemporaries to a degree most unusual for our time. But then so did my parents. Our neighbours, our doctor and many of my father's friends were Protestant. I remember with pleasure that I once avoided kissing the archbishop's ring when he came into a college building at St Stephen's Green. When he entered, everybody dropped to their knees. I didn't do anything dramatic, but repelled, I faded into the middle distance.

I particularly resented the Church's attitude to women. I had at least some instinctive feminist feelings. Two experiences come to mind. When I was about three, my cousin Frank and I had our tonsils out. I vividly remember my uncle visiting us and giving us two jigsaws. Mine had six pieces and Frank's more than twenty. He was six months older than me, but I knew that wasn't the reason for giving me the easy puzzle: it was because I was a girl. And my uncle, a highly intelligent and cultured man, was a schools inspector. Some years later, I went to see the musical *Annie Get Your Gun*. Now the key to this plot was that Annie, a sharpshooter, was a much better marksman than the hero. In the end, to net him, not only had she to 'tart' herself up, but she had to lose to him in a competition. I never got over the unfairness of that: I found it outrageous.

It was extraordinary what women put up with at UCD. When I was there women were not allowed to wear trousers. The Dean of Women Students would send an offender home. And yet we were so obedient that it never actually occurred to any of us to do what was done a couple of years after I left, when hundreds of girls came in one day wearing trousers, and the ban was lifted.

I was aware of the injustices to women but I never had any expectations for myself. I knew that though I was idle I could get through exams but I had no serious ambitions. I didn't know that I was bright and I saw my future as marrying Patrick, assisting him in his career and earning some sort of a living.

Patrick had a postgraduate scholarship at Peterhouse in Cambridge and I got a job lecturing in Liberal Studies and English in a further education college. I was twenty-one and teaching Liberal Studies to sixteen year olds on day release. All they wanted to do was read pornographic magazines and tell racist jokes. I was supposed to be teaching them how to love humanity. I'd show them films about the Third World and they'd fall around laughing. I could see the humour of the situation, but it was very depressing.

I got out (with Patrick's full support) by studying for an MA and getting a first class degree and a prize of enough money to pay my Cambridge fees. Full of romantic notions culled from

Dorothy Sayers I went to Girton. I think I probably visited it half a dozen times. It was full of worthy and industrious women being self-consciously more earnest than their male counterparts. I can be serious, but I am not earnest and I opted for the more frivolous male society of my friends at Peterhouse and Caius. In fact looking back, Cambridge was a very stuffy place — insular, often boring and rarely fun. I liked a few academics — indeed some of my closest friends are university teachers — yet it was obvious that the academic life was not for me. Apart from anything else, I hated teaching.

I spent two years on a PhD on mediaeval history. It was the wrong subject for me. A linguistic moron, I was bogged down in mediaeval Latin. Then I became aware of the world of business. It seemed exciting and I thought I'd join in.

For me, not having children allowed me to make these decisions. I got married assuming that I would have children because there was no alternative. It was postponed for a while and then indefinitely. In fact I never wanted children, though I didn't realise that until later. In my thirties John, my second husband, and I consulted a few people about the pros and cons of having children. My mother said 'Are you mad? You have a great life the way it is.' She said she realised in retrospect that she had had children because it was the done thing.

Patrick and I acquired a ward when she was nine and I was twenty-five. She's my niece and is very dear to me. She was my excuse for a long time: 'Now that I have Neasa, I don't need a child,' but in retrospect I didn't want a baby. I actually like bright kids in late adolescence, when they've got over the horrible stage and are becoming human. I enjoy their iconoclasm, energy and general lack of respectability. John and I found a seventeen year old in 1978, who became our surrogate son. Mick — bright, uneducated, second-generation Irish yet intensely English — worked for me in the civil service. He came to live with us, took his A-levels and went on to university.

* * *

The world is full of women who might not want children but don't have the choice. And my feminism — like my emotional commitment to racial equality — is about the right of people to make such choices. I'm not talking about abortion — which I am unhappy about — but about women's right to use their talents and not be held back simply because of their sex and the social pressure to conform. In Cambridge, I had read Betty Friedan and Simone de Beauvoir. I began to call myself a feminist.

I have several like-minded female friends. We are independent, we like men and we want the same freedoms and choices as they have. In fact (though my friends cover a political spectrum from communist to Powellite), most of my radical feminist friends are, like me, conservative. Patrick and I joined the Conservative Party at Cambridge during the era of the wet liberal Tories like Iain McLeod and Edward Boyle. We were warmly welcomed and I found them a refreshing change from the academics. There was not a shred of anti-Irishness. Indeed because we were Irish they didn't know if we were working class, middle class or aristocracy. Not that it would matter. It is no accident that the Conservative Party have produced the only Jewish and only female Prime Minister, as they will almost certainly produce the first black one. They are short on the rhetoric of equal opportunities but often highly effective.

Since that time I have voted Labour, Liberal and Tory — most often Tory. I admired but did not like Margaret Thatcher. My politics are very close to John Major's — sound money and social liberalism. I am, for instance, passionately opposed to capital punishment.

My feminism was fuelled by the ubiquitous discriminations of the 1960s and the 1970s. I was the breadwinner when Patrick was studying, and yet I couldn't sign a hire purchase form without his guarantee. And when I applied for jobs in business I was rejected several times — unseen — because I was female. (I was also rejected at twenty-four for being too old and over-qualified.) These experiences politicised me. It wasn't like someone telling an Irish or sexist joke at one's expense. Humour — even crude humour — doesn't offend me. But the unfair denial of opportunity did and does.

Eventually I was offered a job in the telecommunications side of the British Post Office where I spent four years. I went in terrified. It was a mysterious world and I had no idea if I was up to it. Apart from the clerical and secretarial staff, the department I joined had up to then been staffed entirely by men who had started out as telephone engineers and come up through the system. I was one of their first graduate entrants. Initially I faced a barrage of Irish jokes to which I replied with better ones — or where I could find them, English jokes. I was despised for being female and therefore useless. But most important of all was the loathing of graduates for the perfectly understandable reason that we were privileged and in a fast stream for promotion. The anti-Irish prejudice evaporated quickly and was unimportant. The anti-female contempt disappeared as one proved one's competence. But the anti-graduate feeling stayed intense and became palpable when some of us were promoted over the heads of people twenty years our senior. All this prejudice was understandable and none of it rankles.

I was excited, experiencing opportunity, attracting attention and seeing a new world of possibilities. My self-confidence soared. I was perceived as keen, hardworking, creative and bright and for the first time I began to see myself in those terms. I even fought successfully for promotion because I knew I deserved it, even though it brought me enemies.

Patrick and I (who are good friends) separated when I was twenty-seven. I wrote my first book during the year after we split up. Through a recommendation from my kind and long-suffering Cambridge supervisor, Geoffrey Elton, I had been asked to write *An Atlas of Irish History*. Living alone in a flat in London, isolated from our friends in Dublin and Cambridge, and with Neasa around only at the weekends, the book occupied me in the evenings. Although I'm convivial, I would rather be alone than be with somebody I'm indifferent to. I dug into the book. I had no desire to move back to Ireland. I was in England forever and I appreciated its scope and freedom.

I was then commissioned to write a book on Patrick Pearse. I took a year off to research and write it. John, an English colleague whom I later married, came with me and was hugely helpful with the research. He became a crucial influence on my development as a writer. In addition to being a brilliant editor of my work, he taught me over the years to improve my style immeasurably. Throughout my life I have had great encouragement from men — my father, husbands, brother, teachers, friends and colleagues. Of course women — particularly my mother — have been important, but until recently there were few of them in positions of influence or authority.

I joined the British Civil Service as a Principal, a relatively senior grade. There were cleverer people than me there, but I could hold my own and I loved it. I was working in the Department of Industry at a time of expansion: there was a Labour government and we were throwing millions of pounds at problems. It was fun and exciting.

There were very few women in the Department of Industry in the administrative class, but we were strongly encouraged by the Permanent Secretary, Sir Peter Carey. He also read my book on Pearse and used to introduce me to outsiders as 'our writer.' The book had been a critical success and in 1979 I had to make a choice between the Civil Service and writing. With family encouragement, but with many regrets and some fears I decided to leave. It was a wise decision: I was probably too much of a non-conformist.

* * *

I had a British passport at this stage though I always described myself as Irish. Yet during the 1970s I had little interest in contemporary Ireland — only in her history. Then I got drawn into the British-Irish Association, became fascinated and began to read Irish newspapers and journals voraciously. I was also going back to Dublin increasingly often. My parents were getting on and I wanted to see more of them. I also had many close friends there. The time came to renew my passport. I spent a month dithering about whether to renew the British passport or get an Irish one. Then there was some appalling IRA atrocity here and I thought I should climb back on, as it were, the sinking ship. If there was a likelihood of Irish people being accused of terrorism, I though it behoved me to stand up and be counted. So I settled for an Irish passport. Perhaps I will alternate every decade.

Much of my resentment had disappeared. Ireland had changed. There was no longer the same Catholic tyranny, the fear and loathing of sexuality that disfigured the Ireland of my youth. At my convent school, Maria Goretti had loomed large. We were told that she was a pure and holy girl who at twelve years old was pursued by the gardener. She refused him his evil way and he stabbed her to death. She was our role-model.

I still feel sad about the way in which generations of Irish people were made afraid of sex through all that life-denying philosophy. Celibacy is fine for those who want it, but it was pernicious to parade it as the higher spiritual goal. The Church made the rules; most of the men were ashamed of their sexuality and made awful lovers and consequently the women hated intercourse. When one looks at it from a distance, the whole business seems extraordinary. I remember John — who is essentially a pagan — looking incredulously at me when I got enraged about some new statement of the Pope's and saying: 'It's beyond me how anyone can take seriously rules about sex laid down by a lot of chaps in frocks who've never had it.'

It's tragic also to think of all those boys and girls who became priests and nuns without knowing what they were doing, and could not get out because of the conventions of the time. It was no wonder that many of them were frustrated and angry. I realised as I got older that vicious Christian Brothers and cruel teachers were usually people who weren't up to the job. If I had become a Christian Brother at fourteen, I might have been pretty nasty by the age of twenty-four. As I understood more about life, I came to terms with the Ireland of my youth.

* * *

I believe that the Irish who look for insults in Britain deserve them. I am aware that we've had our little local difficulties with Britain over the years, but I find it wearying that rather than dealing with the Anglo-Irish relationship now, people still are banging on about 800 years of oppression. Similarly I find extreme feminists tiresome as they hunt out grievances in order to have something to shout about. I find Detta O Catháin admirable. She has had the courage to be an Irish-speaking Tory with a name which the English find almost impossibly difficult and an effective business woman who has never abandoned her femininity. I, who have taken refuge too often in being an honorary chap, have learned a lot from her.

I find the English are remarkably tolerant, very decent hosts. When you think of what they have had to deal with in the last thirty years in terms of the changes in society and the extraordinary diversity of their immigrant population, it is amazing how successfully they have coped and how little gratitude or recognition they receive. Of course there is racism and there are injustices, but England is England; it is in many ways perhaps the most civilised country in the world. It is a hugely compassionate society compared to the one in which I — or most of its immigrants — grew up.

Irish condemnation of British racism makes me furious since Ireland has hardly any black immigrants. And I remember well the rampant anti-Jewish bigotry in my youth, not to speak of the treatment of the travelling people now. I am fiercely critical of hurlers on ditches and as a people we are prone to that — as we are prone to sanctimoniousness; cant and sentimentality. Truth is what I'd die for.

I'm not an Uncle Tom — though I am sometimes accused of being so by knee-jerk republicans. I can be extremely critical of Britain. I often get cross at the English lack of imagination which can cause so many problems in Anglo-Irish relations and the complacent anti-intellectualism of the British people sometimes maddens me. The legal system needs to be reformed; some of the judiciary are boneheads caught in a timewarp; many of the police are prejudiced again blacks, gays and — sometimes — Irish. What happened to the Guildford Four and the Birmingham Six and, worst of all, to the Maguires is horrible. But these injustices did not happen because of institutionalised anti-Irish racism. Like most injustices, they were the produce of ignorance, stupidity and lack of imagination. And there is no country in the world where the law is not frequently an ass and very few countries where the system would admit its mistakes — however disgracefully late in the day.

* * *

I love having two countries and two cultures. You can get the best out of both of them. The Irish bring to the English — who are decent, good, solid and reliable people with many virtues we lack, but a bit on the dull side — light-heartedness, warmth and crack. And that's why they love us and we need them. Despite all the propaganda, the English and Irish like each other better than any two nationalities I can think of. We are greater than the sum of our parts. I wish we could build on this and stop whingeing about old wrongs.

I feel Irish and English to such an extent that when there was that football match between the two countries in the World Cup, I wanted a draw. The same is true in Northern Ireland where I go quite frequently. I don't have a tribe. I went over for the twelfth of July a few years ago to see how it affected me. In fact I felt neither fear nor triumphalism; I simply had a hugely entertaining day. My Northern Irish friends include nationalists and unionists.

I am involved in Anglo-Irish affairs because I hate cruelty and want to do anything I can do to reduce the suffering by helping the two peoples to get on better. The Irish Studies movement is good for Anglo-Irish relations because it helps the English to understand the Irish. Knowledge is always good. Anything that helps to eradicate ignorance is good. I believe in encouraging the teaching of Irish Studies at a level of excellence. It can help us walk tall in this country. We have a magnificent culture — one to be proud of and to share with our hosts.

I have great faith in the new young immigrants coming over from Ireland. They have open minds, energy and a zest for life. I am less happy with the second-generation Irish. Too many of them have romantic ideas about the IRA. Murder, cruelty, destruction and death are not glamorous.

* * *

I was devastated by my mother's death, both by the loss and by my father's pain. She died suddenly in 1985. The next three years trying to help my father cope were very hard. John, Neasa and many friends were marvellous, but the worry was constant.

55

When she died, I thought I couldn't endure the pain but when I came out the other side I was much stronger. I knew I could get through anything: I was never afraid again. Eighteen months later, my lovely father-in-law died of cancer, and then two years later my father died after a short illness: John and I were with him. And a very dear young friend of ours took over two years to die of brain cancer. We were very close to her through all the stages. I think the deaths (and there were others), the strain and the sadness contributed to the ending in 1989 — after thirteen years — of what had been mostly a very good marriage. We still love each other very much.

I believe in the power of love in its widest sense. I have huge reservoirs of affection and that's where I get my hold on life. I feel close to my parents and to friends who have died. I don't think people disappear: I think you leave part of yourself in other people. I used to talk to my mother for a year after she died; it was part of the process of getting through. And I believe that the good you do lives after you: I don't think it gets interred with your bones. I'm an atheist. As I tell Jehovah's Witnesses on the doorstep, 'I'm too charitable to believe in God.' If he exists he has made a shambles of it, and he should go and find himself another job.

Mostly my life is full of interest, joy and fun. Although I often hate the actual process of writing, I love the lead-up and the aftermath and sometimes I get a buzz during composition that more than makes up for the sheer hard grind.

Friendship is central to my life and I am good at it. I trust and love my friends and we give each other emotional sustenance and a great deal of laughter. I have a passion for harmony — perhaps because I grew up in a household of great disharmony. (My parents — both of whom I deeply loved and who were mad about each other — had a stormy relationship.) I need people to like each other, to smile rather than frown, to give each other the benefit of the doubt, to tolerate each other's failings, to pass on compliments rather than criticisms. That sounds pious. I should add that I have a sharp tongue and enjoy venomous, black humour and disorderly, mad Irish nights.

Looking at my break-up with John, I've decided I'm clearly

not very good at being married. I'm too involved in the outside world and I like life to be unpredictable and complicated. I think now, when I look at myself, that I have a terror of being controlled, contained and stopped from doing what I want. If I wake up in the morning and the phone rings and someone says they're just passing through, I want immediately to say 'Come and stay.' I run what friends describe as 'a small Irish Embassy in West London.' I tend to say yes to everything, to grasp the opportunity and respond to impulse. I get work done by shutting myself up for weeks with a message on my answering machine saying 'I'm in Purdah.' But when I finish the period of isolation I break out and head for a prolonged binge in Dublin.

As for marrying again. How would Lady Bracknell put it? 'To lose one husband may be regarded as a misfortune; but to lose two looks like carelessness.' No — no more partners. I benefited greatly from both marriages but now I am wholly contented with a marvellous love affair which brings great happiness to my life. There are great pluses to living alone. You can suit yourself and you can be selfish. I am learning now to be selfish without guilt.

* * *

When I was a civil servant, one of my staff was a Scot. One day I began beating my breast about my guilt at having forgotten to ring someone. He asked 'Is guilt something you learned at University? It's a word you use all the time.' It was the first time in my life I sat down and examined how I used it. It was the good old Irish woman's notion that if you said you were guilty, you were shriven. By acknowledging your guilt it was lessened. And if you didn't feel guilty you were bad. It was drilled into us.

My mother was steeped in it. She died when she was eighty and in the last year of her life I taught her — with difficulty — to say 'I want,' without having to qualify it by 'It would give me a lift,' or 'It'll give me energy to do the housework.' I'm having an interesting time, discovering what I want to do without feeling guilty about it.

I want to go on living in London. I wouldn't be able to cope with the parochialism of Ireland though I love going back, seeing friends and spending hours in the Unicorn and Doheny and

Nesbitt's. But after a few days I feel uneasy because everyone is the same colour and everyone knows everything about everyone else. In London, I have privacy when I want it and contact with many people of many different nationalities. I live in a rich and humane society which I am highly privileged to be allowed to join.

Ruth Dudley Edwards

Personal truths

It's vital for happiness to know how to live contentedly alone.

'Nothing is more unpleasant than a virtuous person with a mean mind.' *(Walter Bagehot)*

'There's nothing worth the wear of winning,
But laughter and the love of friends.' (*Hilaire Belloc*)

'If we owe regard to the memory of the dead, there is yet more respect to be paid to knowledge, to virtue and to truth.' (*Samuel Johnson*)

* The 'marriage ban' prohibited women from continuing to work in the public service after they married. It was abolished in 1973.

Sinéad O'Connor

At the 1990 MTV awards in Los Angeles, Sinéad O'Connor won both best single and best female singer awards. Her first album, **The Lion and the Cobra** shot her to fame in the UK, the USA and Europe. This album has now been certified platinum in Canada and Holland and gold in the UK, Ireland and the USA.

With shaven head, diminutive figure and Doc Martin boots, she spelled a message of a strong, outspoken, independent woman to the world. When singing, her energy level astounds, the soft expression changes, her head moves slightly back and her voice reaches heights and depths that are at once shocking, thrilling, and vulnerable.

In 1989 she made her acting debut in a film entitled **Hush-A-Bye-Baby** in which she plays a fifteen year old schoolgirl whose close friend gets pregnant. Sinéad wrote, produced and performed the entire music score herself. Her single **Nothing compares to U**, a coversong written by Prince, rocketted to number one in the charts in March 1990 and her album **I do not want what I haven't got** followed suit.

Sinéad O'Connor created a storm in America in the summer of 1990, refusing to have the US national anthem played at her concert. She argued that she had to make a protest against a flag that 'says it stands for freedom of speech and then censors the music of black artists because of their colour.'

Born in Dublin, she was the third of four children. Her parents separated when she was eight, and Sinéad went to live with her mother. At thirteen, Sinéad moved back to her father and a new family of three half-brothers and sisters.

Sinéad was married and is now separated. She has one son, Jake.

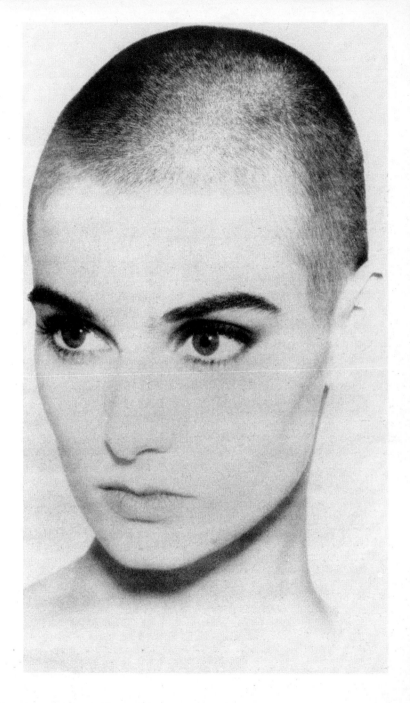

SINEAD O'CONNOR

I AM HAPPY with my musical career at the moment in so far as it is only a particular part of my experience, and my life. My songs are not the most important thing in my life — just a written account of it. I'm happy that it is being documented. If I write songs it's not a separate thing from me; it's an account of what I am.

I'm quite surprised by my success. I didn't expect this to happen on such a large scale, so soon. It's a very confusing state of affairs but also very flattering. I'm especially pleased that the hit record *thing* isn't something that's going to happen to me all the time. I don't want to be perceived as a pop star. I think that leaves you very little room to develop. I want to be perceived as a human being.

Singing was not the most important thing in my life when I was growing up, but I always knew I wanted to do something melodramatic. First of all I wanted to be a ballet dancer, then I wanted to be an actor. I didn't do very well at either of those so singing was the last option. I used to go to auditions but because I spoke very quietly and was very self-conscious, I never did well. You know the way you are supposed to project your voice and reach the end of the hall. I was miserable. And in my ballet, I was just not very disciplined. But my mother encouraged me to try out all sorts of ways of expressing myself. I always loved singing, especially hymns. I sang a lot in the choirs at school and at Holy Communion ceremonies.

I didn't like school very much as I grew older. I had hassle from teachers for expressing myself. As an Irish girl in school I was expected to comply with rules, to do as I was told, to believe what I was told. I was forbidden to dress differently from society's view on how women should dress. I couldn't cut my hair the way I wanted — you know, in a way that wasn't expected and I had to make sure that my top button was buttoned at all times.

When I was fourteen I was caught stealing and I spent eighteen months in what is called a residential centre for girls with behavioural problems. That was an interesting experience. It was good in that it stopped me stealing, but what I feel now and what I felt at the time was that somebody ought to have got to the root of the problem rather than just trying to cure its manifestation. The stealing was obviously caused by the fact that I was fucked up. Ireland has a great habit of not getting to the root of the problem and just pushing it out of sight.

I felt that I was being pretty much pushed out of sight and that nobody was actually interested in finding out what was wrong with me. I went to see a very famous Irish child psychiatrist, with my parents. Instead of trying to find out what the problem was, he just sat there and told me my parents' opinions. He told me I was a problem child and I must listen to my parents and do what I was told. I think that is quite shocking.Where children are disturbed, it's important for the psychiatrist to keep in contact with the child for a long part of their lives. They should know the child and at least investigate what life is like for that child. They need to understand the circumstances which may have pushed them into drugs, drink, stealing or bunking off school or whatever it is. A lot of this anti-social behaviour is a result of problems at home. I should not have gone to see the psychiatrist with my parents. I could not express myself freely with them. If I had seen him on my own I could have talked to him, explained a little of what was going on for me. As far as I was concerned, it was just a case of him getting paid fifty quid for an hour. He didn't really care what the problem was.

Basically, I was stealing because I was confused. My parents were separated, and I grew up in a very stern, restrictive home when I was living with my mother. She was a huge influence on me and still is. Her life as an Irish woman wasn't very satisfied or fulfilled. It was more a case of me looking at her and deciding that I didn't want to end up like that. And that I must leave. I must also make sure that I express myself. She is more an inspiration for me from that point of view. It wasn't that I modelled myself on her. I decided that I would be what she had the potential to be. Living in Ireland she could never be happy.

When I went to live with my father, suddenly I had freedom, I had pocket money, I could go out. I had never had freedom before and I didn't know what to do with it. I didn't believe that stealing was wrong. In fact people around me encouraged me to do it, so I didn't see a problem with it.

It was a huge relief to leave the residential centre. I went home for the summer holidays and then was sent to a liberal Quaker secondary boarding school in Waterford. It was an OK school, but since it was in the country and more conservative than Dublin, young women were expected to wear white socks and skirts and behave themselves. I had this sort of punk hairdo and I used to wear a padlock round my neck, and there was my leopardskin trousers. I had a very hard time from the staff and some of the pupils. I was ostracised and bullied by some of the male students because I didn't fit into the stereotype of what they thought a woman was supposed to be.

The next summer I returned to Dublin and decided that I wanted to sing. I put an ad in *Hot Press*, a music magazine, saying that I was looking for some action and I joined a band. I had a great time with them. When I had to return to school I was completely depressed. I had finally figured out what I wanted to do and I felt it was a total waste of time being at school. I asked my parents could I leave and they said no. So I tried to get expelled by smoking because usually if you were caught smoking three times in a row you were thrown out but that didn't work, so I woke one morning and decided to leave. I went up to Dublin and joined a band.

I'm not determined but I think I'm very lucky. I'm an impulsive person and I act and live very much on my instincts and my impulses. When an idea has come into my head or into my stomach or wherever, I have gone for it and it's turned out alright. I know I'm capable of doing the things I want to do.

* * *

I was sixteen when I came back to Dublin. I was completely on my own. I had to get myself a bedsit. It wasn't that I decided anything, it was just that's what I had to do. I wanted to be a singer, and I didn't know why. I just knew I wanted to express myself, I wanted to express everything I felt. I sang with the Tom Tom Macoutes band for about a year, but then things went a little sour. A record company, Ensign, came over from England to see us around the time we were splitting up. They said they liked the singing but didn't much like the band. Then we split up. I didn't really know what I was going to do. I thought maybe I was going to end up doing the pub circuit singing *Summertime* for the rest of my life. I wrote to the guy at the record company and told him I had been offered a record deal and asked him for some advice. I was just chancing my arm. It worked. He rang me up and said 'When are you coming over?'

I was glad to leave Ireland, glad to get out. I was never so happy in my life as the day I got on the plane and I never ever have looked back or missed it. I hated the place. It's the most depressing place in the world for me because of my circumstances growing up. I just can't deal with it unless I'm completely drunk. Going to London meant freedom, it meant escape, it meant I was 'out' at last. This was the lucky break I was waiting for.

It was only when I started out on this road that I began to see that being a woman in the music business does put you at a disadvantage. It would be a lie to say it doesn't. People don't take you as seriously and they're very patronising to you. At my first disagreement with my band Ensign, I blew my top with them so they have never taken me for granted since then!

I've also been very lucky in my choice of managers, solicitors and accountants. All the people who work for me in these capacities are very good friends. They understand me artistically as well and therefore I'm never in a situation where my integrity could be compromised.

I was very homesick in my first few months in England. I

stayed for a while in Greenwich with my Aunt Martha. My record company gave me some money when I signed the record deal and I got myself a flat in Lewisham. I was put there with an acoustic guitar and told to write my album.

So I sat there for a year and I didn't see anyone, except a Jamaican minister who I was having a torrid affair with. A married man. I met him at my Aunt Martha's house. He was forty-seven and I was in love with him. He was my first big love. I was naïve, because looking back he was a total wanker. He was married with children nearly my age, he was a religious minister, he had responsibility for young people, so what was he doing with me? He gave me a Valentine's poem once and it was a photocopy and it had 'Dear ....' with my name filled in. I wondered how many others he had sent. But he provided a reason for me to stay in London. If it hadn't been for the fact that my heart was in London I don't think the rest of my body would have stayed there. It's a cold city. People are not very friendly.

* * *

I was broken-hearted after my affair with the minister ended. I met John on the rebound. I was pregnant a month after we started going out with each other. My pregnancy was a huge problem for the record company. Their doctor told me I shouldn't go through with it. The record company had spent £120,000 on recording my album and he put pressure on me to terminate my pregnancy. I 'owed it to them to have an abortion,' he said. I was raging and devastated. They filled my head with nonsense in order to frighten me into getting rid of it. The doctor told me that if I went on a plane it would damage the baby, and that it wouldn't survive my jumping around on stage. As it turned out, I never went on tour until Jake was about six months old. They pressurised me to the point where I did actually go into hospital to have an abortion, but I changed my mind and just sneaked out again. It's interesting to note that, at the same time, a male singer being promoted by the record company found out his girlfriend was pregnant. Nobody said to him 'You musn't have a child because we've spent a lot of money on you.'

I was so ecstatically happy to be pregnant. The first time I ever clapped eyes on John, though I never fancied him or was never in love with him, I said to myself 'There's the father of my child.' I was happy for myself. It meant I had somebody to keep me company, and I was going to get loads of attention being pregnant.

I found the whole birth experience very frightening. I was completely terrified. I didn't know it was going to be that painful. It took me a year to get it out of my system, and it took me a long time to appreciate Jake. I felt uncomfortable with motherhood for a long time. I was only twenty. I thought I was a grown woman, but twenty is very, very young to have a baby. I was still a child myself and still growing. It's only now that I'm building up a really great relationship with Jake. I didn't have any spiritual feeling giving birth; quite the opposite. But I have had loads of other spiritual experiences.

I would love to have more children. I'm obsessed with children. I love being pregnant and I love babies! John was very supportive. At first I think he was very frightened of having a baby. We'd only been going out for a month but once he saw how important it was to me, he was always very kind. He's a brilliant father.

* * *

I don't know where you go when you die, but I know you go somewhere. It's all far too vast and incomprehensible, isn't it? I got interested in other worlds when my mother was killed in a car crash in 1985. I started going to see mediums. I got into tarot cards, yoga, numerology, cabala and so on. I went to the spiritual association meetings. It's not that I wanted to contact people who had died, but I wanted to learn about the universe and why it exists and what our role in the universe is and what God is.

Spirituality is about realising that we are God, that human beings were made in the image of God. If we are God, then all the things that we are capable of doing and realising and reflecting and learning are part of our function in the universe — to reflect God.

I believe that a person chooses their life, and the work that they want to do in the world, throughout the course of their life.

They choose before they're born, the parents that they're going to have, the upbringing that they want, the things that are going to happen to them, their emotional experiences, the love affairs — in order to learn, to acquire certain traits and become the person they are going to be in order to do whatever work they're supposed to do here.

I've lost my Catholicism. The Church has made a lot of mistakes in interpreting the information that it's been given in the form of the bible. It's not just Catholicism, but Christianity as a whole which has been responsible for the wiping out of women feeling pride in themselves. It has been responsible for making women subservient. Society used to have powerful women running countries. There were goddesses, and mythological religions were for the most part based on women, but Christianity ended all that.

The Catholic Church also has blood on its hands, the way it has accumulated riches as a consequence of butchering people up through the centuries. I think the Church has frightened people off their sexuality. I still have problems as a result of growing up in Catholic Ireland. Certainly through most of my adolescence and even up to six months ago I was very inhibited. You were brought up to believe that sex is something dirty. If I was making love to somebody I used to feel really guilty. If I liked it I used to think that I was really horrible. As a consequence I have a real hard time having sex with somebody I like. I don't associate it with love. I almost think that it's something bad.

As a result of being told that sex is a sin and dirty and wicked, I understood that the woman's body was something to be ashamed of, so I'm not that comfortable with my body at all. I find that I'm sort of stiff. You're not brought up to be a woman in the Church. You're not brought up to be proud of being a woman, and feel womanly, and do womanly things and think womanly thoughts. You're brought up to be subservient.

I had an experience recently where I was very physical with another woman. I wouldn't do it again because I'm not interested, but I'm glad that it happened. I liked an awful lot of things about it and I learnt a lot about being a woman and about women.

Since this experience I have felt much more comfortable with women, while before I had a problem relaxing with women or being friendly to them.

I think the Church can bring you up to believe that it's wrong to feel affection for anybody, but especially for anybody who is the same sex as you. That it's wrong for women to be physically affectionate with each other which, of course, is rubbish. This makes you think that because you feel physically affectionate towards a woman it is because you want to have sex with her, but that's not necessarily what it means; it means that you want to put your arms around her. But you're brought up to believe that the physical expression of love for a person of the same sex is wrong.

I have a whole group of women around me, and also my husband John, who support me. I married John on the rebound from someone else. I felt I should get married in order to make myself happy and that this in turn would make John and my son Jake happy. I'm not married anymore. We've decided that we didn't like living together as man and wife and we'd rather be friends. Marriage is a very unnatural situation for me. It's great for some people, but not for me. I found that although John was a very unusual husband in that I never lifted a bloody finger, I didn't feel comfortable with the idea that I couldn't be with anybody else. I got married when I was twenty-two, which was stupid. I think you should wait until you're about fifty.

There aren't people queueing up to go out with me. I thought there were going to be, but there aren't! It's made more difficult when you are famous because you don't know whether they're only chatting you up because you're famous. I'm not a normal girl. Men are intimidated by me. There are the ones who wouldn't go within a five mile radius of you because they're completely frightened and then there are the ones who are only interested because it's Sinéad O'Connor. Living as a single woman can be tedious, but there's the occasional ship passing in the night!

* * *

As a woman I've had a great time in London. I've had my share of trouble being in a chauvinist business, but socially I've had a great time. My friends range from musicians, film-makers, fashion designers to my accountant.

I've never felt conscious of being Irish in Britain except once when some geyser came up to me in a club and asked me was I Irish and I said yeah and then he said 'Are you Catholic?' and then he sort of tutted and walked off, but I just thought he was a prick, it didn't affect me.

I think of London as my home more than anywhere else in the world. There was a phase when I thought of Ireland romantically, looking at it as a thirty-two county Republic. I think I was naïve and I certainly don't think a bit of land is worth fighting for. It has to be acknowledged that the British should never have gone into Northern Ireland in the first place. It's not right to invade a person's country, to take away their culture and their language. But the answer is not to go round blowing them up. I think all people who live in Northern Ireland have a right to be there. To say that some have no right to be there is the same as saying that the black people have no right to be in England or that the Irish have no right to live in Britain. I would like to see all sides in Northern Ireland talking. I don't know if this would solve it, but I think that communication and discussion would be the way to start.

* * *

Fame can disorientate you and affect the way you communicate with people near to you. Having done so well with *Nothing Compares to U*, my number one hit, and just finishing my world tour, I realise that it's a hard job to remain balanced in such a chaotic world! Fame and world tours can damage you psychologically. I feel very disordered.

During a nine month tour, you experience about five years' worth of life. Something different happens every day and something traumatic happens every day. You realise that people are very manipulative, very dishonest. Some people will do anything to further their own ambitions, whether they're sexual or financial, at your expense. It puts you in a position where you don't trust anybody and you think everybody is lying to you. You get to the stage where you just can't tell any more who is honest and who isn't. And then you end up having a low opinion of yourself — you start to dislike yourself because you're so obnoxious, not trusting people! I find the spiritual reading I do roots me at these times. I don't like the word spiritual, but it's anything that I read that inspires me. It recharges my batteries.

For the future I would like to have more children. I would like to be an actress rather than a singer, but I will continue to make music. Growing up I was angry and my music reflected this but now I am a young woman and my songs are different.

Personal truths

I would not be a man for the world. They have the hard time. Women are very lucky.

Women have a lot of power and we need to get in touch with it.

Ainna Fawcett-Henesy

Ainna Fawcett-Henesy was born in Limerick. She emigrated to England to train as a nurse in 1965 and is a qualified midwife and community nurse. She is now Regional Director of Nursing to South East Thames Regional Health Authority. This is an administrative position in a region which has more clients than the entire population of Ireland.

Before taking on this major new job, she was Chief Nurse and Director of Quality at Ealing Health Authority in London. While there, she acquired substantial money to develop a research project into the views and involvement of consumers in the health care system. She introduced a major nursing quality assurance programme and a Nursing Development Unit, the first in the region.

Ainna was also adviser in Primary Health Care to the Royal College of Nursing where she took an active role in promoting the leadership role of nurses. She is currently doing research for a doctorate on this topic and has always been committed to the value and breadth of the nursing vocation. During her time with the RCN she played a major role in negotiating for a review of Community Nursing. She led the nursing deputation at the Secretary of State's travelling seminar on Primary Health Care, 'An Agenda for Discussion,' and negotiated with the British Medical Association and the British Pharmaceutical Society for the ability of nurses to prescribe drugs.

Her impressive range of activities includes membership of the King's Fund Carers Forum, the Royal College of Nursing, the Curriculum Development group for the Nurse Practitioner course, External Examiner to the Health Visitor Course at Oxford Polytechnic and she was a member of the Department of

*Health Working Group 'The Health of the Nation.' She has travelled abroad on study tours in America, India and Japan and in 1986 won the Florence Nightingale Scholarship to study leadership in primary health care nursing in Canada. Ainna Fawcett-Henesy is an experienced public speaker, and has also written for a number of publications in the nursing field. She is currently Associate Editor for **The Nursing Times**.*

Ainna Fawcett-Henesy is married, has no children and lives in the country with her husband. She loves entertaining and tries to get to the theatre at least once a week.

AINNA FAWCETT-HENESY

I HAVE the top nursing job in the South-East Thames Region, which stretches from London to Dover. There are 37,000 nurses working here and I'm their leader. It's an executive job. I sit on a board with other professionals, and plan the future of health care for the whole region. I wanted this job, though I have a further step to go. I have planned out my career and this is part of my 'critical pathway.'

I always wanted to be a successful woman. I was absolutely sure that I wanted to succeed in my chosen profession and I have a tremendous drive to achieve. Not in a ruthless way because whatever step I have taken I have believed so much in that step. I felt that this is so important, I must do it. Before this, I was Chief Nurse of Ealing Health Authority. I went to Ealing, set my objectives and achieved them. I didn't want to leave as early as I did, but circumstances changed. I saw this job advertised and thought I stood a very good chance of getting it. I feel I'm as good as anybody else — in fact I feel that I have more to offer than most, given my experience.

I suppose I get most of my drive from my father. He believed in himself. I wouldn't consider him the most successful of men since he actually went bankrupt but he had a tremendous enthusiasm and zest for life. Drive for me is about zest for life rather than something solely for your career. My father was a very colourful excitable man but tough with it.

My drive is also about succeeding in a male-dominated society. At home I had two brothers and one sister and the emphasis was very much on the boys. I feel I've succeeded

75

despite that lack of encouragement. The rest of the family had their jobs sorted out for them by my father, and I was the only one to leave home. There's nothing like Ireland for nepotism. There you can succeed without really trying.

I'm from Limerick; my mother is from the country and my father from the city. I have lots of negative feelings about growing up, though there are some positive ones too. On reflection, the world is in fact a much nicer place than I thought but certainly Ireland wasn't so nice for me when I lived there.

Our family environment wasn't a very positive one, for all my father's zest. My parents argued a lot and engendered a good deal of guilt in us children. I was the typical stereotyped little girl, who played with my dolls and played house. I can remember getting a nurse's uniform when I was about seven or even younger. My father was good at providing the material things but less good about the loving and caring aspect of parenthood. He thought that you could be successful as a woman only if you were a nurse or a teacher. When I first thought of being a nurse I was petrified, but I knew it would please him. It wasn't a case of having a nursing vocation. In fact, there were times when I wanted to run away from the idea but I was frightened of my father's displeasure. That was a strong feeling for me. My father was fine until we started to assert ourselves and started to stand up for our rights. He didn't like that. He loved us when we were little, but he didn't want to be challenged.

My memories of school are quite bitter. I went to a rather select school called The Model. There were very clear class divisions at our school between the 'haves' and the 'have-nots.' I always considered myself as one of those who had, although not as much as some who had more. I remember there were twins from a poorer area of town. One morning they were both afflicted with a bout of diarrhoea. They were treated like lepers and sent home, in a cold, unsympathetic way. If they had been from an uppercrust house, I'm absolutely sure they would have been treated differently. The class system and the nepotism in Ireland are wrong.

It suited me to be part of the 'in crowd,' the privileged crew. While I think it didn't mean much to me at the time it disturbs me in lots of ways now, and probably my choice of career is linked to these early memories.

I hated the nuns. I loathed and detested them. I'd love to go back to my secondary school and say 'Look how well I've done.' I don't mean it in an arrogant way but I would emphasise 'You should give everybody the best chance.' The school was The Mount, a convent run by the Mercy nuns. I was this little plump girl, and that was how I perceived myself, though I think I've improved with age! But there were two families who were always singled out for attention; they were perfectly groomed. If you weren't in that league or from the right part of town you were dismissed. I remember standing back, watching and noticing this and knowing that something was wrong. I had a conscience even then.

My father encouraged us to have a conscience. For all his faults, he was a generous man and would give his last penny away. It wasn't because we were affluent, but there was that thing about 'giving away' — sharing.

He owned a large newsagency which included a post office. I often helped in the shop. I can remember going in and opening up when I was about fourteen or fifteen. I'd get the shutters down and start the business for the day. I'd collect the accounts door to door. My father had a huge circle of contacts and his company was always lively, animated and great fun.

My mother was the opposite. She was quite subservient and, sadly, she had all the traits I hate now. She was a country woman and rumour has it that my father married her as a second choice. His family certainly didn't consider her to be his equal, socially. My mother was hard and strict, and so was her mother. Though I admired our grandmother more. She could assert herself; my mother couldn't. My mother was reserved. Whereas my father would welcome the world, my mother didn't like people around; she wanted her own privacy. I love company, the opposite of my mother. I think she was always annoyed with my father for his friendly ways. I can now appreciate just how difficult it must have been for her, given her nature.

I knew I had to get away from home as my parents were rigid and strict. If you kissed a boy you were 'cheap.' Really, I didn't have a social life in Ireland. I wasn't allowed out to my first céilí until I was eighteen. I was told to be home at half past ten, and when I arrived at the door at eleven, I got walloped. Being walloped was not an unusual occurrence in our household. If you were home late, you were out to get yourself pregnant.

In retrospect, I suppose, it was pure fear of sex. My mother had a horrendous time because of the ban on contraception. She was terrified of getting pregnant. She waited in trepidation for her period each month, a fact she confided to me in later years. Nobody should be subjected to that amount of fear. Though I criticise her, I can rationalise now and understand that she had a very raw deal. I often wonder if it was her fear that turned her into a strict and unhappy woman.

I remember I had saved up money to go on a trip to Stratford-on-Avon, Shakespeare country. I loved acting, and had paid my fare myself. When she found out, she forbade me to travel. 'Over my dead body,' she said. This was also the stage when my father would come with me to shop for clothes. I was allowed little freedom. My friends were often disapproved of.

I was almost ready to have my first period when I asked my mother about it. She told me it was not the right time to discuss such a private subject. When she did tell me about it, I cried all night. It was a horrible experience. There was nothing joyful about growing up. There was certainly nothing to celebrate in this new world opening up to me. The period seemed a curse that was to befall you for the rest of your life.

Of course everything was hidden. Sanitary towels had to burned at the dead of night. I can remember stealing down the stairs so that nobody would see them. As for tampax, you couldn't even look at those in the shops; they were most definitely sinful and guaranteed to ruin your womanhood.

If you looked at a boy you were in trouble. It was as if sperm could run up your leg and make you pregnant. I can remember the first time I actually kissed a boy. I was sixteen. We went to the pictures and I came out with discoloured lips. I was so scared that my mother would guess what I had been up to that I bought an ice-cream, hoping that it would hide the discolouration.

I just knew I had to leave home to survive. There was no

question of me going to university when I left school. I can remember my father saying 'You'll get married and have children, right?' Though when I said I wanted to be a nurse, he pulled out every stop to encourage me.

I had an interview for the Regional Hospital in Limerick. There were people my father knew on the board. I had my hair done in a real sixties look, turned out at the ends. I wore this bright pink suit with a navy blouse. I thought I looked terrific. When I arrived in, they asked me why I wanted to be a nurse. I replied 'Do you know, I'm not that sure!' I remember deciding that I was going to tell the truth and not give them the usual 'Oh, it's because I care about people.' I wasn't selected and there was furore at home. 'Who'd give you a job looking like that. Sure you look like a street-girl.' My justification for not being appointed was because there were 144 applicants for four vacancies. In later years I thanked God I wasn't offered that job, because I would have had to live at home, which would have been dreadful.

My father really suffered, He was embarrassed and angry that his daughter had not been selected. Then it was decided that I would train in England, where an uncle of mine was on the board of governors at a Warwickshire hospital; he could 'keep an eye on me.' My father made an advance trip to the UK to prepare the way for me! He drove us all up to Dublin. I had a new dressing gown and suitcase. It was a parting of the ways. I was very frightened.

When I got to England I took a bus. I wasn't sure of where I was going and this man on the bus was very kind and told me where to get off. I eventually found the home sister, who gave me a cup of tea. They had no supper that night because there was a hospital ball on, so I was given a can of soup. But there was no opener to open it. I had come from a very protected home I couldn't believe the contrast that night as I sat on my case sipping my tea. I cried all night and thought, I don't want this life, I really want to go home. I sobbed. I had never felt so alone as I did then.

But I settled in. There were other Irish girls there, and that made it easier, though I had been so cushioned from the class system that training with women from very different backgrounds to my own was quite a shock for me initially. I enjoyed the crowd I trained with; they were down to earth; we had great fun. I was certainly one of the lively ones, and a leader. I grew up in all sorts of ways that first three years.

I met my first boyfriend Chris, my first love. When I went home on holidays, he wrote me a letter, which my father confiscated. There was a lot of prejudice against the English in Ireland in those days, and my father was quick to point it out.

Another time I returned home with my hair dyed blonde. Only that I had brought home a friend, my father would have turned around and left me at the airport. He ignored me the whole holiday, except one afternoon he persuaded me to take a trip with him to the local sausage factory. The hooter went at one o'clock, and all the young female workers trooped out with rollers in their dyed blonde hair. 'See,' he said, 'that's what you look like. Take this money and get your hair changed tomorrow.' I refused. I kept it blonde; that was me growing up.

When I met my husband Clive, a non-Catholic, and told my parents about him, they were horrified. Clive's parents were equally displeased that he was proposing to marry a Catholic. They wrote and said that I was no longer a member of the family. I met Clive on a blind date. He was gorgeous. I was very sure of him and knew I wanted to marry him. It was ironic that even before they met him my family didn't accept Clive. The first years of my marriage were difficult but I didn't feel able to ask my family for support. I felt that I had made my bed and I must lie in it.

* * *

I am a Catholic and I do practise. It's actually a very important part of my life. I would have to admit that there's a guilt element about it. If I didn't go to mass on Sunday I would feel guilty on Monday. I would feel that things would go bad for me for the week!

Clive is the total opposite to me. He doesn't have this sense of spiritualism. He believes that it's a prop, but he has always encouraged me in my religion and often reminds me that it is time for mass. He has no difficulty coping with Catholicism, but has often had a problem with my being Irish and has encountered prejudice. When he says his wife is Irish, he has been made to feel uncomfortable, although this is beginning to change now.

I've manipulated the Catholic code to suit me. I took the pill, and don't believe that anyone should be dictated to with regard to a moral code. I am driven by a desire to empower people, not take away their choice. Contraception should be an accepted norm, and divorce should be allowed. They are fundamental human rights. But because the Church forbids them, it does not mean that they are all bad. I don't feel hard done by because I grew up a Catholic. It's important to me, even if some suggest that it is a prop. I feel it gives me a framework for my life.

The trail of Irish women coming to England in the last moment of labour to hospitals over here was a standing joke during my training. You know, 'Here they come, the poor Irish off the Euston train.' It's a tragedy. No country has a right to treat its women like that. I used to feel embarrassed on the one hand and so sad and sorry on the other. I came from a middle class background where I was taught to believe that I was somebody, but these Irish women were a standing joke among my fellow professionals. It was a tragedy that these women gave birth to babies who were promptly put up for adoption because they fell into the single motherhood bracket. I just wondered whether Ireland felt any responsibility to its women.

It is the same now with the droves of Irish women coming here for abortions. I am grateful that they can at least come over here, that they don't have to suffer having a child that Irish society doesn't want because a church-led state has made rules they must abide by. Being a nurse was a training that opened the injustices of the world on my door step and which I had previously been unaware of.

* * *

Death was the one reason I didn't want to be a nurse. I was terrified of it. I hated laying patients out. I fear death. But I do think there is a life after death. There is definitely something. I've an idealised view of death that I learned about when I was a

81

child and I've never changed that image.

I've often dreamt about dying, that enormous drop and suddenly you wake up. It's an area I block out. I've been ill a few times when I've been overcome by a fear of death and I have become quite panicky about the thought of dying. I can remember dreams where I've been lifted up. Thankfully I have more dreams where I am going to heaven than hell!

My father died of cancer at quite a young age, as did my mother. I was at mass when the news of my father's death came through. It took me a long time to get over it. My mother's death from cancer was tragic. I was the nurse in the family and was expected to be there and be the strong one. I was working in a high-powered job with the Royal College of Nursing but my brothers expected me to be by my mother's side, which I did, as much as I could.

Deep down my mother felt she was worth very little. She lacked so much self esteem, she kept saying what a wonderful daughter I was and that she didn't deserve my care. I was in the middle of making a film at the time on primary health care teams and had to be back in London. My mother asked me not to leave, she said 'Please don't go,' and I had to go back to England. It broke my heart. She slipped into a coma after that and she never said anything else to me. She died three days later. I was there when she died, and I laid her out. I had to do it. It was therapeutic. It was as if I was persuading myself that at least I could do that in the face of the powerlessness of death. It was awful. I had terrible nightmares after that for a long time.

It's a relief that my parents are dead because at least the phone is never going to ring again with that news. I don't feel as close to the rest of my family, and I don't live with that same fear.

* * *

I'm a workaholic and in a way it helped me cope with my mother's death. I'm up at quarter to six and don't finish work until nine in the evening. I do most of my creative thinking at work. I don't have children. It wasn't a conscious decision. I just never got pregnant. We both went for tests but as my career began to develop it just wasn't a priority. Sometimes I wonder what it would have been like. I know I would have made a good mother but I don't feel deprived. I have a nice home, a great career, some good friends. I horse ride and read. Clive has never objected and I suppose if he wanted children he could go off and marry someone else to have them. He is a wonderful man and he would move mountains of earth to help me. He admires my stamina and style. He is proud of my achievements. I am lucky. There could have been an unwitting thing of him not wanting me to succeed and not burning the midnight oil with me. But that was never the case. It's a good partnership.

I edited a primary health journal when I was at the Royal College of Nursing and he often stayed up late into the night stapling articles and licking envelopes with me. I've always loved writing and am an associate editor of *The Nursing Times*.

The media has promoted me and my cause. I have said things that nobody else dared to say about nursing. Any time the media wanted a quote, they rang me. I was invited on study trips to Japan and America with the press of Fleet Street. I was promoting a much wider role for nurses as Nurse Practitioners, prescribing drugs. Everybody thought it was outrageous, but we have it now. I was visible and outspoken.

People invited me to speak and write. I challenged the medical profession on the role of nurses. I am a bubbly sort of character so I was liked and invited back again. I also had achieved. I wasn't just talking, I was actually doing as well. I took risks, made decisions and broke new ground.

After taking a degree at the open university I enrolled for a PhD which will be on leadership and nursing. I want to promote nurses, not as leading from behind but out there in front. Irish nurses are respected here for their caring and their sense of duty but I also think it's important to see nurses in a strong, assertive, independent role and not just bowing in deference to a medical hierarchy.

/ I know I couldn't have had the opportunities I have had here if I had stayed in Ireland. There was freedom for me here in Britain. I was a free spirit. Away from my family I had a chance to mature. My confidence grew.

I love going back to Ireland. I used to lecture in Northern Ireland and when I was there I would take a trip to Dublin. I loved Northern Ireland and had great times there. The Northern Ireland question is certainly an issue which touches all our lives. I believe in the powers of negotiation and how important it is to get all sides talking.

Most of my job is about change management. You start small, pick a few leaders, raise their self-esteem and awareness and then send them back into the community to infect others. Working with leaders is key. We have evidence that people can work together and in Northern Ireland Protestants and Catholics do. There is no reason why change management principles cannot work in the political world too. There is discrimination everywhere, but negotiations must always start with a dedication to equal opportunities; although I wouldn't underestimate the work ahead for negotiators in Northern Ireland.

I would be happy to return now to Ireland to live. However, I would not be bound by restrictive rules. If I wanted to divorce, for instance, I would return to England.

I feel I have established a life in England which is very different from that in which I grew up. Yet I haven't abandoned my heritage because it's very important to me. Being Irish means I belong to a rich culture which I am very proud of and which I believe has contributed enormously to my achievements and success.

I am at peace with myself, yet I have a hunger for new challenges and a desire to help others to succeed. England has provided me with many opportunities which ironically my Irish background has facilitated.

Personal truths

Believe in yourself, whatever the forces against you; believe that you can do it.

Be honest with yourself when you're taking risks and in your relationships.

It may sound awful now, but tomorrow morning it will be less so.

Deirdre Duffy CJSP

Deirdre Duffy CSJP is a Catholic sister aged fifty-one. Born in the West of Ireland she spent her teenage years in Northern Ireland. She moved to England in 1957 to start her religious training with the Sisters of St Joseph of Peace in Rearsby, near Leicester.

She is currently co-ordinator of the Conference of the Major Religious Superiors of England and Wales Social Justice Desk. This body represents all religious, male and female, in England and Wales, about 14,000 members. The Desk was instrumental in determining the focus of the Conference in 1990 as 'a prophetic voice of the poor' — a radical change in focus.

Deirdre worked as Disarmament Co-ordinator for the British section of Pax Christi, the international Catholic peace group. In this capacity she participated in many international conferences including the First UN Special Session on Disarmament in New York, the Women's UN Conference in Copenhagen, the Non-Proliferation Treaty Review Conference in Geneva, and the Conference for Representatives of World Religions in Tokyo. She also attended conferences in most East European countries prior to the collapse of the Berlin Wall.

Committed to justice and peace issues she has worked with ex-prisoners, drug addicts, homeless people, the unemployed and single parent families. A qualified AIDS counsellor she finds time to work on a part-time basis with those living with the HIV virus.

She has been an active member of many different bodies including the Radio Leicester Religious Advisory Panel, the Nottingham Diocesan Northern Ireland Committee, the Bishops' Nuclear Issues Committee, Pax Christi National and

International Executive Councils, and International Peace Bureau Executive Council.

Always warm, generous and caring, it's not surprising that she is known throughout Britain for her work. (She has undergone major surgery this year, but has bounced back with her usual enthusiasm for life). She actively promotes social justice issues at workshops and conferences, many of which fall at the weekend. Despite the heavy work load she still manages to spend some quiet time with friends.

A qualified music teacher, Deirdre loves classical music concerts and the theatre. I interviewed her at her office in Central London.

DEIRDRE DUFFY

MY FAMILY BACKGROUND is a mixed one — English and Irish, Catholic, Anglican and Presbyterian. Because we were from the South and because we were not politically involved we made friends with people regardless of their circumstances. Some of my friends were not Catholic and therefore other Catholic friends dropped me!

My father worked in the bank and the family was transferred from the West of Ireland to Northern Ireland when I was in my teens. People didn't speak to us; they didn't serve us in some of the shops in Banbridge. It was the late fifties and at that time a lot of cinemas and electricity stations were being bombed. You felt that people looked at you with suspicion and we were frequently stopped and questioned by the 'B' specials.

We used different doctors. Some of the family went to a Catholic doctor and others to a Protestant one. During July, because of all the Orange Order fever, we were not accepted by the Protestant one because he would not speak to Catholics, even patients, in July. During this month the lambeg drums often beat outside our door and every Sunday the orange band would play 'God Save the Queen' outside the chapel during benediction.

There was a Young Farmers Club which did not allow Catholics. My sister was determined to join up. My parents backed her all the way and she did join, though the local priest criticised her.

I found it difficult to understand how people could hate others, not knowing what they stood for — not accepting them as people. I think that is when my sense of injustice started. I have been concerned about justice issues since I was a teenager. I have always been conscious of discrimination.

I was angry at the divisions in Northern Ireland, although my father discouraged me from getting politically involved. It's hard to understand now but I found it very difficult to cope with Northern Ireland. I wasn't really aware of the injustices but found the whole scene emotional. When I left it for religious training in England it was like leaving part of myself that I couldn't understand behind.

I first felt that I wanted to be a nun at the age of twelve. I wanted to go on the missions. I was accepted by another congregation but then I realised that it was the Sisters of St Joseph of Newark that I wanted to join. They used to come into the bank where my father worked and he knew them. When I told these sisters that I wanted to become a religious they never once said 'You must enter with us!' They never questioned me, they just accepted me and let me make up my own mind. There was no pressure and that appealed to me.

There were two sisters of this congregation in Cabra outside Newry and they had a strong influence on me. I think it was the fact that they could integrate holiness with being human. They were not of the 'holier than thou' kind. They were aware of world problems, and they were caring, warm, friendly people.

My father did not encourage me to enter though my mother accepted it. I think she was quite pleased to have a religious in the family — it's a respectable Irish tradition! But my father was not happy. His concern was that I was always a determined person — if I said I was going to do something whatever it cost, I did it. And he was afraid that I was just determined to enter because I had said, at the age of twelve, that I would. He retracted that in later years and realised that it was the right thing for me.

I am one of three children and my sister was terrified that I would try and persuade her to join up! I was very close to my brother. He was very upset that I was entering but in later years I know he was proud of it. He also developed the same views on justice that I have. He wouldn't even allow his children have a water pistol or any other war toys.

Leaving for the English province of the order was a big separation. And though I wasn't the eldest I was the first to leave home. But I quickly settled in and just accepted it. It was something I knew I had to do. I was at peace doing it and that was important.

* * *

I first trained as a secondary school teacher. At that time I didn't give much attention to oppression or injustice. The first school I taught in was a primary school in Nottingham and I was involved with families from the financially deprived areas. Then I moved to Yorkshire where there were many social problems among the different ethnic communities. I became extremely conscious of the oppression of many of the students coming to school without any breakfast or adequate clothing and how this affected their ability to learn. In many cases there was violence, poverty, drug addiction at home. I was part of a group which co-ordinated a scheme for teenage girls, many of whom were pregnant and on drugs.

I found myself becoming more and more aware of the injustices in the educational system. It was exam orientated and did not cater for those who had difficulty with the English language, or who came from homes where academic achievement was not a priority — or even a possibility. Our job was to fill heads with facts and figures and it just seemed to me that people were being depersonalised, that their dignity and human value was being overlooked. I was struggling against that.

After ten years teaching I took a year out and went back to Ireland to St Patrick's College in Maynooth and did theology and philosophy — a renewal course. I then returned to the Nottingham diocese to do social work with single mothers and babies. There were many single mothers and once again I was made aware that the 'system' worked against them. We could support and help people but once they went back out they were numbers and they had few to stand beside them. If they kept their child they had to cope alone in bedsits. There was very little support.

I began to feel this growing awareness of the 'haves' and the 'have-nots' in society. If you could not speak for yourself, nobody listened or cared, nobody wanted to know. We live in a divided world — where the silent minority exist in oppression and poverty, marginalised and made to feel unimportant. They have no voice, no power and are considered useless burdens to society.

I applied to work with Pax Christi, the international Catholic peace movement. My initial work was on nuclear disarmament issues. This was leading up to the United Nations special session on disarmament. The more I got involved in this work the more I realised the inter-relatedness between it and the work I had already been doing. We had a large number of poor people, homeless, unemployed, struggling minority groups but we could still spend about £8 billion on defence in 1977. We currently spend £21 billion a year on defence and that does not include the cost of the Gulf crisis.

I knew of a medical project which had been developed for diagnosing diabetes. It would have needed one million pounds to set up and half a million pounds every year to run — it meant early diagnosis but the government was unwilling to spend the money on it. The whole contradiction of this appalled me. We were so involved in production of arms that we didn't care to whom or how they were used. Once they have been sold we have no control over them being re-sold. There were virtually no restrictions on the sale of arms. We would sell them to Belgium and they could sell them to someone else and, in fact, there is some evidence that the IRA were using British-made weapons to shoot British soldiers! The whole arms race represented a blatant denial of gospel values. The dignity and quality of life are not important provided the country has status, power and visibility in the rest of the world.

I was sent as a delegate to the first special session on disarmament in the United Nations in New York. My whole spectrum of the debate was widened. I was in my thirties and met many delegates from around the world including victims of Hiroshima. I spent a lot of time studying treaties and documents relating to disarmament and information coming from the

Vatican. It was obvious that many who had signed arms agreements had broken them.

In the early days I was one of the few religious and certainly the only Catholic woman religious at these international conferences. I was a novelty and perhaps because of this I was invited to many other international meetings. I had a chance to travel and meet other cultures and broaden my own personal horizons. I thoroughly enjoyed this challenging ministry and the many opportunities it presented to promote the gospel values of justice and peace. I, personally, felt very at peace with the job, though it was a rather unusual one for a religious in those days. Now, very many religious are involved and doing tremendous work in the varied areas of justice and peace.

I travelled around parishes in Britain informing parish and other groups of the great injustice of stockpiling arms. I tried to draw attention to the commandment 'Thou shalt not kill.' If we call ourselves peacemakers it is wrong to support policies where our government is promoting weapons of mass destruction.

I have identified myself as English, or at least accepted that the British government is my government at the moment. I knew from the very first day I arrived over here that I was going to live according to these structures and in my early days I accepted that everything that government did was right. I of course also accepted that everything the Church said and did was right! I now feel differently and tend to question much more.

The Falklands war cost this country a phenomenal amount in financial terms not to mention the deaths, injuries, disabilities, the aggrieved families and the whole wave of right wing nationalism which grew up over night. I began to look at government structures and what they were doing and realised that some of our structures are a denial of human dignity and human rights and create a huge 'rich-poor' gap in society.

As part of my work with Pax Christi we liaised with government officials. I was present at several meetings with Ministry of Defence officials and the Minister himself. We also met with bishops. I never went into a diocese without meeting with some of the clergy and getting the permission of the local Bishop.

* * *

I feel a great pain about the whole question of Northern Ireland. I have a sense of empathy with the people who are being discriminated against whether they be Catholic or Protestant. I have sympathy for those who have been maimed or who have lost their lives, the number of innocent who have been caught in the cross fire, the number of army and police who have been unjustly killed. I think my great frustration is that I cannot see a solution.

Though Pax Christi is involved in Northern Ireland I never got involved in this work. I realised how angry I felt about it all. I just couldn't be objective about it. Changes in Northern Ireland are going to come from the bottom upwards and I feel concerned that some of the initiatives (like the integrated schools), which have come from the bottom are being criticised by the Church. This saddens me. Surely it is with the young that one starts to try to break down prejudice — they learn it and are indoctrinated with it by the example of their elders.

I would never live in Northern Ireland again but I do return there. I have relatives in the Republic and in the North. But if I had no family in the North I would not visit. I find the bitterness, the anger, the discrimination, the whole sense of uneasiness there difficult to handle. I do not feel at peace there. I do not feel enough solidarity with the people though I do have deep compassion for them.

I think the solution has got to start with the children growing up. And a gradual withdrawal of British troops should be planned. What a lot of people have failed to understand is that this is not a religious question. It is a culture problem, a clash of two cultures. The people in Northern Ireland have suffered from people from other countries and cultures going in to Northern Ireland, having a look around and saying 'Right, we have the answer,' then setting up projects destined to fail because they have never understood the problem in the first place.

It's got to be left to the people of Northern Ireland to say, 'Right, we have two cultures. We respect yours. You respect ours.' Maybe we could learn something from Britain. We are trying to co-exist here in a multi-cultured society, accepting different traditions.

I have been welcomed here, and I have never been discriminated against because of accent. There are a great many Irish sisters which is comforting but I am not that conscious of people's nationality any more. When I go home to the Republic, though, I am struck by the friendliness and the openness of people. What saddens me there is that whole missing age group who have emigrated. Ireland has its fair share of problems — drugs, poverty and homelessness — so I don't see it all through rose-tinted spectacles.

It's evident that there is a great move away from the Church in Ireland. I'm not surprised. I think it's because the Church has been so tightly structured there. We need to understand the Church in a much wider context. It's not a hierarchical structure — it's about the people of God.

* * *

After my work with Pax Christi, I was asked to help co-ordinate and prepare a social justice programme for my own Order. Our motto is 'Peace through Justice.' Our founder, Mother Frances Claire Cusack, has had a great impact on my life. Anglo-Irish, she was first an Anglican sister until she became a Catholic and entered the Sisters of St Claire in Newry. As a novice she was sent to help make a new foundation of that order in Kenmare.

A prolific writer, she wrote on the lives of saints, and a history of Ireland and books of advice for young girls. She was a public figure and spoke out against the injustices to the poor in Ireland and the plight of young girls denied education emigrating to America and England with little chance of work and ending up as prostitutes. She eventually founded her own order in 1884.

By this time she was a controversial figure because she publicly criticised the hierarchy of the Church who were often paid by the English absentee landlords and who were isolated and separated from their flock. She started her Order in England and then moved to America to set up homes for Irish girls. Many of the bishops refused to meet with her because of her courage in being so outspoken and political. She was seen as a trouble-maker. In 1888 she could see the suppression of her sisters by the Church hierarchy and felt that it was she herself who was perceived as the rebel. She felt that her Order was the will of God but that she must leave for it to survive. Mother Frances returned to Britain where she continued, despite failing health, to give lectures. She decided to leave the Church, she was so disappointed and frustrated by her inability to bring about change.

I admire this woman. There was a lot of unresolved pain in her and I think she led a painful life, but I can identify with her. I can identify with her vision and her understanding of Gospel values, what her aims were and what she wanted to achieve. That vision, for me, means standing against the system and looking at the structures that create injustice, which often involves taking a public stance. We have had some sisters imprisoned for their stance against nuclear weapons or for protesting against the evictions of Puerto Ricans in America.

I have never been arrested though I have taken part in many demonstrations, including the protest at Greenham Common, where women drew the attention of the world to the immorality and pointlessness of nuclear armaments. These women achieved a lot. Like all movements, a few fanatics joined on and I would not agree with some of their policies.

I think that women are going to be the ones who will bring justice and peace to our world. Part of the reason why the world is in the mess it is in at the moment, with the destruction of the environment, the rainforests, the ozone layer, pollution and so on, is that the feminine aspect of creation has been suppressed down through the centuries — in the sense of recognising the qualities the feminine could bring to leadership in governments and the contribution women can bring to society and Church. We have lived in a male-dominated Church, a male-dominated society. Men have seen themselves as controllers and masters, not stewards and caretakers. I do feel the feminine qualities of compassion and listening and empathy are emerging and not before their time. It is a long, slow and often painful process and struggle.

I don't see men as the enemy; in fact I like men! My male friends however are men who do not see males as the dominant sex in society. They are open to giving women their place in the

Church and in society. They are compassionate men who are
concerned with justice. In fact most of my friends share my
value system.

* * *

Looking back on my life as a nun, the hardest time was in those
earlier years because you were not really encouraged to have
close friends. Now we can have friends, male and female.
There's more warmth, support, affirmation and sharing in our
religious community. We can think and talk in a mature and
healthy way about sexuality without fear or without thinking that
it's wrong to do so.

Now I understand that as well as the vow of celibacy having
to do with sexuality, it has to do a great deal more with a
commitment to our mission. It's about reaching out and loving
the marginalised, the oppressed in our community, being open,
listening, sharing, caring, being free and having the time to do
this. It has to do with freedom, wholeness and integrity.

I do love children and I get on extremely well with them. I
have no regrets though. If I were given my life to live again I
would not change any of my choices.

I see the day when there might be married priests but not
married nuns. There is no need for married sisters; there are so
many married sisters in the Church who are doing our work and
on many occasions doing it a great deal better than us.

Like sex, spirituality was something the religious did not talk
about in the older days. You had your prayer times, you did
those and that was it. If you had a spiritual director you might
have discussed the choice of personal prayers with them but
other than that you really didn't talk about what your prayer was
all about. God for me was someone up there in the sky, a man
with a beard to whom I talked at certain periods of the day and
then I got on with my life. Now I have no problem referring to
God as 'she.' God doesn't have to have a sex though, because
God is far greater than our minds can understand. God is in the
in the flowers, the trees, everything that is beautiful. God is no
longer in the Church, in the tabernacle; God is everywhere — in
the inner-city ghettos, in the polluted air, in the poverty ridden

countries, in the pain of Her/His people as well as in the beauty of creation.

My whole concept of spirituality is widening and widening to integrate everything in my life, in society and in creation. If I go out and share a meal with friends that is an aspect of spirituality. If I work with people with AIDS and if I spend time with them, that's also an aspect of spirituality. Every action that enables growth in my life is a spiritual action because human beings are integrated beings — not separated compartments making a whole.

* * *

I stay in the Church because I believe it is the Church founded by Jesus Christ. I believe that I am the Church and I have the right to criticise injustices and to try to create the Church that I think Jesus meant when he instituted it — embracing everyone. A Church which does not discriminate against anybody, which promotes love, unity, true compassion, justice and peace.

If life in the next world is a continuation of this one I will be quite happy! There is a place for everyone in life. Nobody is born by accident and there is a role for everyone. The society we live in is a very selective one which says that certain people are right, that a chosen few have a role to play and others don't. I believe that we all have a contribution to make.

I had a lot of illness as a child and I have often thought about death. I have no fears of it. I think I will be with God in the next world and with my friends.

I am much more aware of social sin rather than personal sin. I lead my life to the best of my ability but my big frustration at the moment is my contribution to a social sin. In my personal life I can try and relate well to people, to acknowledge their dignity but by living in this society I am contributing to social sin every day and sometimes I feel I can't do anything about it. I'm part of a structure which is creating marginalised, disadvantaged people and I'm one of the privileged. As a religious I am privileged. I have the freedom to go on retreat every year, to have time to pray. In my work now as Co-ordinator of the Justice and Peace Desk of the Catholic Major Religious Superiors — a body which represents nearly 14,000 religious, sisters, priests and brothers in England and Wales — I have been instrumental in encouraging people to realise this privilege.

I am delighted that many religious organisations are joining with other like-minded bodies to create social change — to create a society where the dignity of the person is recognised, putting resources into providing for quality of life rather than preparing for war — a structure that would look at its gross national product not just in terms of wealth and wealth equalling money but wealth equalling the gifts and variety and quality of its people.

When I first came to Britain there was definitely greater equality and more even distribution of resources. There wasn't such a gap between the rich and poor. Many of the national health services were better and there was a feeling that the future was manageable. Today the National Health system is completely threatened, state bodies have been privatised and the increase in personal tax has created a great deal of insecurity among people.

One of the things that strikes me most is the increase in numbers of suicides in recent years and the number of people I meet who don't have a sense of the future. Many of my values are socialist. True communism is actually the gospel in practice! It's equal opportunity for all, equal distribution of resources to enable everyone to live with dignity. That's what I'm about, it's what my ministry is about and why I feel so committed to it.

Personal truths

Whatever happens, God loves me and, if I let go and love God, whatever I was created for will happen.

Don't be afraid of where you feel God might be calling you because you think you are lacking the gifts for that situation.

Moving from ministry to ministry I found I had the necessary gifts. Our potential is much greater at times than we think. (*Deuteronomy* Chapter 29: Verses 19-20)

Detta O Catháin

Detta O Catháin, OBE at the age of fifty-three, is one of the top women in business in Britain. She was head-hunted for her present job as Managing Director of the huge City of London arts complex, the Barbican Centre. She is responsible for 250 permanent staff and 600 contract workers.

Born in Cork, she is the eldest of three children. She was awarded an OBE in the New Year's Honours List in 1983 for services to agricultural marketing. She emigrated to England in the mid-sixties to join her future English husband. Working as an assistant economist with Aer Lingus, she quickly moved up through the business world, becoming a director of Market Planning for British Leyland, a corporate planning executive with Unigate plc and the Managing Director of the Milk Marketing Board.

She currently holds non-executive directorships of Midland Bank plc, Tesco plc and Sears plc. She has also been a non-executive director of Channel 4 TV, a member of the panel of judges for the Prince of Wales Award for Industrial Innovation and President of the Agricultural Section of the British Association for the Advancement of Science. On 30 April 1991 she was created a Life Peer and hopes to take her seat in the House of Lords in the near future.

She is delighted to be working in the arts and sees her business experience as vital for successfully marketing her product. Her first year on the job has not been easy with the resident Royal Shakespeare Company closing for four months during the winter to save funds. She faced this possible crisis confidently and competently.

Married for twenty-two years, her husband Bill suffered a

stroke eighteen ago months which meant permanent nursing and a move from their old house to a more convenient one in Arundel. I interviewed her in her three-bedroomed high rise apartment in the Barbican Centre, just two minutes from her office, where she lives during the week. She spends weekends in Arundel caring for her husband. They have no children.

She loves music, literature and politics. Gracious, charming, interested, she likes order and feels a personal responsibility to make things right for everyone.

DETTA O CATHAIN

WHAT I MOST LIKE about my job as Managing Director of the Barbican Centre in London is that it is in an area that I never thought I would be involved in, an area I'm passionate about — the Arts.

Since I was a very small child I've been interested in the Arts. I've always been a great music lover and concert goer and suddenly here I am with this great complex under my belt. It's terrific. Music has always been a passion. I appreciate it. I don't play a musical instrument even though I took piano lessons for ten years! Fortunately I married a man who is a brilliant pianist, or was before his stroke. When I got married there was no way that I would sit down and 'tinkle the ivories' because he was so good.

I was born competitive. There were three children in the family. I wasn't competitive with my brother and sister — both younger than me but I remember being competitive with my peers at school and also competing against myself. I set myself extremely high targets.

As a boarder in Laurel Hill convent, in Limerick, there were rewards for study on Sunday mornings. We were encouraged to work and study, and to go beyond the realms of what we were learning in terms of reading around a subject. Of course you had to work hard. I remember being stuck in a study hall for many hours with the eagle eye of a nun at the top desk.

Those school days left a mark on me to a greater extent than my family. The teachers encouraged me to do things for what I found out later were all the right reasons. I was shown the reason why I should behave in certain ways whereas at home I was a strong individual personality without much concern for others. In school I had to 'play ball,' I had to be a team member. I honestly think my management style today comes from the team building that I experienced at school. I have an open management style and team building is very much a part of it.

I wasn't encouraged to be an individual at home but I just was! I feel I am quite different from my mother and father though I look quite like my mother now and people say I speak exactly like her — an old university friend of my mother's says I even write like her. My outgoing nature comes from my father's gregariousness, friendliness and very natural attributes. My mother was reserved — she was English. I think I have the best characteristics of both races.

My mother was a strong personality. She was very determined, much more so than my father. She was a 'stayer' and when she got it into her head to do something she would stick by it. My father tended to be more Irish. He'd take up subjects with loads of enthusiasm and then drop them, whereas my mother would doggedly keep at it. If my mother decided to learn a foreign language she would keep at it until the day she died.

England featured in my childhood as my mother's family still lived here. I used to come over to Britain to visit my grandmother during and after the war. England was always good and better — far away hills are greener and all that. You could get Mars bars in England. Even then I was 'consumer aware.' I loved the choice of things in the shops. I used to go window shopping in Birmingham. I liked the efficient way that England ran. I was impressed with the life here.

The war was exciting for a young child. I was born the year before it broke out. Images of wartime remain clearly with me. The lights, the sirens, the drama, not that it was horrible or awful. I never thought of people being killed. Although I saw a lot of bomb sites and found them frightening, I knew of nobody close to me who had been killed. The war didn't really bother me. I led a sheltered life.

My father was a senior civil servant, and the money in the family was spent on private education for the children. After this hefty bill there wasn't much left. When I think of the money I spend now I really am shocked. It was a very careful household and even today I hate to waste anything. Yet I do waste, buying convenience food. I somehow see that as something of a let-down of my own standards because, first of all, I should be capable of concocting a proper meal, and, secondly, it's extraordinarily expensive when you look at the ingredients and you think what you could do with a little effort. But then I rationalise it on the basis that after all, I work very long hours and I don't have the time to cook and I don't have the opportunity to do shopping. If I was living at home being a full-time housewife, I wouldn't buy convenience food.

I have a drive that I must do everything. I think it's because my self-confidence isn't very high, which may seem strange. If I can bake a super cake or a *tarte à l'oignon* that means I can do it, I'm not stupid — that's my reasoning. It's in the doing rather than in the achieving that I value myself. I'm very task-orientated and I like to do things well.

I was a prefect at school and was always in the top three of the class. I was regarded as being bright and capable, but lazy. I remember an old teacher ranting and raving about my lack of real application and she was right. I'm certainly not lazy now, not idle at all. I wonder is it because I'm so programmed in my life that there isn't time to be lazy? I often wonder if I didn't have the sort of job that I have now, would I fall to pieces going around with my heels worn down and looking scruffy? I don't think so. My hefty working schedule is part of me now; it's become a habit.

* * *

The teachers at my school have left an indelible mark on my memory. There were three particular nuns that I remember — strong characters, real people. They could laugh and joke. They weren't just narrow nuns relating to our religious education. They were women and people of the world. They had lived abroad.

Though the nuns did encourage devout, Catholic, religious practice, I didn't find it overbearing. By nature I'm a dogmatic person. I could have gone either way in my youth, being completely religious or irreligious. There were not many half-way points for me then. I was not a compromiser. I was a black or white person, though I must admit I'm more grey now, literally as well as belief-wise. I see the benefits of holding back and not being too dogmatic about a course of action.

One of the things which marks me out from other people is my quickness in seeing through things, getting to grips with them and grasping answers. Because of this, I am often at the end when the rest of the team are only half-way there. This can lead to impatience on my part which is not very clever because it can put people off and create problems with their lack of self-esteem.

In the very act of rushing through something you can tend not to think things through quietly and carefully. Now, at my advanced age, I have come to realise there is a middle way to get there and get to the bones of things, while holding back a little so that other people can get involved.

I had no indication when I was growing up that I was going to enter the world of business and administration. There was never any real emphasis on women doing anything. It was assumed that you would marry, have kids and be a good wife for your husband.

I was very unsuccessful with boyfriends but I had great daydreams that a man on a white charger would arrive and take me away to live in a beautiful house where I would live happily ever after.

Those things didn't happen. Unattractive I might be, but I knew I was blessed with a brain. So I decided to study and continue to use it. It looked like the only talent I had got from God.

I started to work in Aer Lingus when I left school — the travel aspect of the job appealed to me. I started as an accounts clerk, which didn't much please me, but I made the most of it. I would have liked to go to university after school, but didn't know what to do. My parents had pointed out that I was the eldest of three and if I went on to university and wasn't sure what I wanted to do, it would be a waste of time and would jeopardise the financial chances of the next two coming up. Pressure from home pressed me into making the decision either to go to university or earn a crust of bread. I did both. I stayed on working at Aer Lingus and financed my way through university, attending evening classes, studying economics. Windows of opportunity opened for me. I took the promotion and the chances. I do think you make your own luck to a large extent.

I met my husband Bill at this time. He's English and he worked for Aer Lingus in the Birmingham office. I didn't initially think he was the man for me. He was utterly charming, good fun, and very self-assured. He was very masterful, a trait I admire. He fell for me in the biggest possible way. I was flattered by his attention. When someone really loves you and they show it, you either fall for them or you don't. I fell for him.

There was no question of expecting him to join me in Dublin. His career was in England and he was also a divorcé. Marrying a divorced man in Ireland would have been awful. As it was, my parents didn't speak to us for two years after we married.

Bill's concern, care and love really sheltered me and cocooned me as I separated from everything I knew. He showed me affection that I never had before. It wasn't that my parents weren't affectionate but they weren't demonstrative. Bill made me feel terrific and I had never been made to feel terrific when I was a child in case I got a big head. I don't remember my parents praising me. They'd say 'Oh well that wasn't bad.' I always felt that my brother and sister were brighter than I was.

Intellectual ability was the all-important marker in our house. Both my parents were graduates. My mother graduated in 1932, when there weren't a lot of women graduates. She was a standard bearer for education, very bright and there was lots of reading in our house.

The few boyfriends I had were categorised on a dim/not dim scale. Meeting Bill was like a breath of fresh air. I moved over to England to join him in 1966 and we lived together for two years before getting married. It was not the accepted thing to do but since Bill's divorce hadn't come through, we had no option. I was swimming against the tide. Not very many people knew about it; we didn't flaunt it. People in the community where we lived thought we were married.

I was sure of his feelings for me. I made a strong commitment to him and he did to me. We made it work. It hasn't been without problems but we've made it.

We married in a registry office. We couldn't get married in a Catholic church because of his previous marriage. I was upset because of my religious heritage and believed that I was now a lost soul. I'd committed a mortal sin as far as my Church was concerned.

I was deeply religious in my youth but my whole belief system was shaken up when I met Bill. I stopped going to church after we married. Then I began to realise that God is a loving God. Love is the main gift from God to man and somebody who loves you isn't about to throw you into the flames because of your own weakness. It was this fire and brimstone approach to God which I remember about Catholicism.

I knew people in Ireland who were pretty evil by any conventional measurement — who were 'crawthumpers', going to mass on Sunday and then slandering people's character on Monday. I just couldn't understand it because none of us is perfect. They were treating other human beings in a way which was completely contrary to anything that Jesus taught us in the New Testament. The hypocrisy appalled me.

I did feel an emptiness not belonging to a Church. I need to belong to a particular congregation not for the sense of belonging, but for the implied discipline that it gives in terms of making time for God in my life. Without an allotted time for God I probably would forget about my spirituality. I became a member of the Church of England. I have been accepted there and welcomed. I really don't understand abstract concepts of spirituality. I've had to make my God a person. I have to stop and think and will myself to talk to God.

Certainly my faith comes from my family background and my school and Ireland. We were brought up to believe that anyone who was not a Catholic was doomed, that, in fact, their life would be hell. When I started to question my religious beliefs I began to think 'What on earth were these Catholic missionaries doing bringing their western ways to Africa? Converting a people to the Catholic faith when the Africans had their own fine beliefs?' I realise that God commands his disciples to go out and preach the gospel (and, by inference, 'save souls') but I find it difficult to accept that missionary zeal is always to the advantage of Africans.

Imagining an after-life, I hope that I will be able to meet my friends there and be happy. Occasionally I have moments of sheer bliss and I think that is what it will be like. I can't see the purpose to being here if there is not an after-life.

* * *

Getting married to Bill was a very natural progression in a happy relationship. At the time I got married I couldn't have imagined myself not being married but if I had my time over again, I don't think I would have got married. I'd like to have lived with Bill permanently, as it is more acceptable now. In marriage, you can become a bit of a possession and I don't like that. I support the independence of the individual. Being independent has always been important to me.

I made a conscious decision not to have children. Bill went along with that; he has two children by his previous marriage. I don't actually like children. I'm sufficiently like my mother to have been a similar mother and I think she resented children. She resented them getting in the way. I wouldn't have the job I have now if I had been a mother. I couldn't possibly have managed a senior job and bringing up children. There's something in my brain which is triggered off by the sound of crying children; it's absolute torture. I don't like mess, slop and muck all over the place, toys everywhere and you can't sit down to a logical discussion with someone because you're interrupted by a couple of kids. I have some goddaughters and I like them, in small doses.

There was pressure put on me to have children, thankfully not from Bill. It was tough, but it's *my* life. I don't dictate to you whether you should have children or not. Nobody should dictate to me. It's up to those who want them to have them and I just couldn't bear the thoughts of it. I believe the world has too many people in it anyway. Let those who are good parents create replacements for the rest of us because if we all keep procreating the way we are, there will be too many people on the planet.

My marriage is a much better one for not having had children. There are the millions who stay together because of the kids and they loathe one another. We stay together because we are committed to each other, not to the kids. I've seen parents take their resentment out on their kids and these children in turn continue this cycle of abuse. I have seen far too many people annihilate themselves psychologically by having kids and sticking together. A pet hate is going out to dinner and tentatively asking how the children are. You open the floodgates and you have to listen to half an hour of it, and I'm saying to myself I'd much prefer to talk about a concert I was at. I'm just not a mother.

* * *

Sometimes I really don't think I'm good at anything. Looking back at my career, I am surprised. I have this idea that everyone in the world is better than I am. I look at my personal assistant. She has a terrific personality, she's glamorous, efficient, a great typist — I am no match for her. What people recognise in me is just sheer hard work and good management style.

I took the opportunities that came my way. This is connected to setting yourself targets and achieving them and looking for tougher targets and achieving them and all the time improving yourself and your knowledge base and skills. At board meetings, I would listen, do my preparation. I realised that everyone else thought I had a contribution to make; they believed that I should be there.

It's important, genuinely, to support the organisations that you work for. I did. I was interested in them and I had lots of ideas. I have been around a long time and there is nothing novel about business systems. I mean they change but the basic principles are the same.

We all need to confront male harassment. You have to point out that you find the behaviour objectionable; on the basis of sheer logic show the harasser that you are light years away from him. I have had to do this. Smoke them out. If they continue and are still taking advantage of you, there is the legal route where you can take them to court or else you can chuck the job. I would. I'd chuck a job of £100,000 a year (if I had it) and go and stack shelves for a while. I just wouldn't put up with harassment. I've never been afraid to move either, if things were not working for me.

I was awarded an OBE from the Queen in December 1982 for my work in agricultural marketing. Peter Walker, the then Minister of Agriculture appointed five 'lively minds' to generate ideas for the improvement of marketing British agriculture and food products. I was working for Unigate. We came up with a lot of ideas, one of which was the launch of the Food from Britain Campaign. I guess people in the ministry regarded me as being reasonably bright and my name was put forward to the Prime Minister, Margaret Thatcher, who in turn recommended me to the Queen.

It was other people rather than myself who were more pleased with my OBE. My father was thrilled to bits and so was my husband Bill. With time it has grown in my estimation. It's not as great as some of the other honours but it's something. I find now I use it more. When I came to the Barbican Centre all the advance publicity stated that I had an OBE and they had visiting cards and letter-headed notepaper with Detta O Catháin, OBE, Managing Director. It now seems much more a part of me.

* * *

I look up to Margaret Thatcher and the Princess Royal for sheer dogged determination, achieving and working hard against all odds. Both of them are women of integrity. I admire them enormously.

I am very worried about the state of Britain at the moment. It's a very difficult task to get this economy right. It's like pushing water up a hill. There's an innate laziness and idleness in the welfare state attitude which I find distressing. But politics is, by its nature, partisan. The scoring of cheap political points is pathetic. When you speak to politicians on an individual basis, confidentially and off-the-record there is very little to choose between good people on either side — Tory or Labour. But put them into Westminster and they sometimes appear like kids squabbling over silly things.

I blame whole systems for the troubles in Northern Ireland. I blame the education system, parents' attitudes, everything. I pray to God that sense will prevail. There has been an enormous amount of bad judgement, bad management, bad decision-making on both sides. The rampant violence and terrorism actually physically makes me sick. I'd love to see peace where people treat people as people. It doesn't matter what religion you are. If I were living in Northern Ireland I imagine I would have to find out, and the pressure would be on me not to speak to you if you were from the other side.

This is such a wonderful world, amazing sunrises, wonderful sunsets. When I return to Ireland I often stand still and it overwhelms me, with the peace and quiet, and I think just below the skin there is this festering evil, hatred; it's incomprehensible. I feel totally powerless against it. I have got drawn into various British-Irish Associations to counteract this but the immense insoluble nature of it is overwhelming.

There is definitely something indelible about being Irish. There is a Celtic notion which for me is vaguely romantic, slightly risky, a little irresponsible, carefree, with time for people, beauty and creative pastimes. I don't parade these attitudes — particularly in the business world where I have chosen to work, they don't mix. I wouldn't return to Ireland. My home is here. I do not see myself retiring for quite a while. When my husband had a stroke there were some suggestions that I should. I'm making half-promises to Bill that I'll give up after this contract is up in three and a half years' time. I don't know if he will be alive at that stage. He is very fit but I do know that these things take their toll. If he's not, I wouldn't contemplate retiring. I'd do something else.

I suppose the high point of my life at the moment is that I have the best job in the world and the low point is that I wish I had had it twenty years ago.

Detta O Catháin

Photograph: Apertures

Personal truths

Love Thy neighbour.

To thine own self be true; thou cans't not then be false to any man.

Once you take a decision, particularly about your own life, you take the decision and you never say 'I wonder what would have happened if I had gone the other way?'

Miriam O'Callaghan

*Miriam O'Callaghan was born in Dublin thirty years ago. She is the second eldest of five children. A solicitor, she started a career in television when she emigrated to England in 1983. In seven years she moved rapidly through the broadcasting ranks, starting as a researcher on **This is Your Life** with Thames TV, then becoming reporter with BBC's **Out of Court**; senior producer on **Kilroy** and both presenter and producer on **Primetime**. She is currently reporter on BBC's **Newsnight**, a prestigious investigative current affairs programme. She has chosen an unusual television route, working as researcher, producer, presenter and reporter. She believes in learning and acquiring a variety of skills.*

Married to writer and broadcaster Tom McGurk she has one daughter, and lives near Shepherd's Bush in London. She prides herself on being organised. Any spare time she has, she likes to devote to her daughter.

Her interests are politics, the piano (she has a diploma in music), Van Morrison, women's rights and Dublin pubs. She loves returning to Dublin, where she has a fond relationship with her family.

I met Miriam at the BBC Television Centre. Nearly six feet tall, confident and friendly, she lead me to the Current Affairs department. This is her second home, and the ability to work in a close knit team is a quality she carries with obvious ease. Unashamedly enthusiastic and curious, she has a serious side, and an earnest desire to do her best in every aspect of her life.

Her desire to communicate is coupled with an analytical, diplomatic streak. She says what she means clearly and concisely, and rarely looks back.

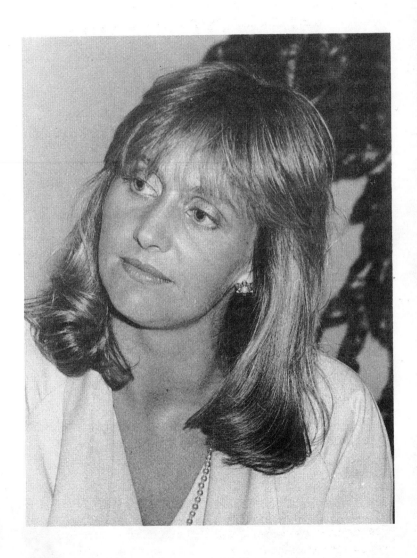

MIRIAM O'CALLAGHAN

I OFTEN WORK a seven day week. Being a reporter on BBC2 *Newsnight*, you need a full-time commitment. I am also a producer and I've worked as a presenter. Being a presenter and producer is a very unusual combination. Gay Byrne does it at home. With these two branches of skills you can end up with quite a lot of power! In fact, on a job it is probably better to be either a producer or presenter; being both means that you miss out on a pooling of ideas. But I chose to carry both jobs because of the temporary nature of the media business. If someone gets sick of your eyes and you're the presenter, you can be ousted. In this work you are very dependent on the whims of editors. I've seen how it works, and very good people can get the push because somebody new comes along and decides 'No, I don't want her on my show.' This doesn't happen as easily when you are a producer. It is definitely more secure. My parents always drilled into our family the importance of a pensionable, secure job. My mother was a teacher and my father a civil servant. They were conservative, in a good way.

I think you are drawn to television if you enjoy meeting people and hearing new ideas. Our family life was full of debate, congregating in the loo to discuss the latest controversy. I am the second eldest in a family of four girls and one boy. The four girls never shut up. My parents were strict in that we were not encouraged to play on the street and when we were young we very rarely went out. I think we really learned from each other and became very close.

My elder sister Margaret did forge ahead and break family

rules and regulations so that it was easier for the others growing up. She was very intelligent and a little unconventional. I was always the goody-good and she was always bold. Living in Foxrock, on Dublin's southside, stealing out for a dance when we were in our early teens was nearly impossible. It would have to be planned months in advance. Margaret would be up on the appointed Saturday washing the dishes, frantically hoovering the house, bringing my parents breakfast in bed, so that we would get permission to go out!

This whole rigmarole was good in a way, because it made getting out really special. My parents were very protective, very straight and very happy. My father did not expect girls to get married. If we had no boyfriends, he didn't care. He encouraged us at school and supported us at university. He didn't have the opportunity to go to university himself but he wanted his daughters to go. All of us did and that's a credit to both my mother and father.

He was brought up on a farm in County Kerry. He was almost a feminist in his views on what women should do. He didn't raise us for the traditional Irish female role of motherhood. He does not care that my older sister Margaret, who is an academic, has not tied the knot. He just does not think it is relevant.

My mother was a most important influence in all our lives. She came from a small village in County Laois and was determined to succeed and escape rural Ireland. She became a teacher and although she had to give up her job because of the marriage ban,* she returned when the law changed. She became a headmistress, which was unusual as most of the top jobs in teaching went to men. She was an inspiration to her five children, and all her daughters assumed that as women in the world, we would work and get on in our careers.

My mother, though like my father in some way, is like many Irish women — no matter how much they take on new ideas they still worry about their daughters if they aren't married. Neighbours at home who know us never say to her 'That was a brilliant project your daughter was involved in.' They ask 'Are

* The 'marriage ban' prohibited women from continuing to work in the public service after they married. It was abolished in 1973.

more of them married yet?' or 'Any new grandchildren?' That seems to be still an important criterion of success or failure for women in Irish society.

It is because of my parents that I believe we all ended up with very good academic qualifications and in really interesting careers. Margaret, a historian, was a Cambridge Don for many years and now lectures in Queen's University. Anne is an extremely successful public relations executive and Kathleen is a journalist in London for *The Mail on Sunday*'s 'U' magazine. Jim is the only boy and the youngest, but he luckily managed to survive his four sisters and is now a post-graduate law student in Cambridge and is also a fine rugby player.

I went to the local national school where my mother was headmistress. She was strict on us — there was no favouritism. I was then sent out of the neighbourhood to a secondary school, Mount St Anne's in Milltown. My parents felt that the local schools were too snobby. There was a much wider mix of students in Milltown. That was important for my parents. It was unfortunate in one way, though, in that we completely lost touch with local girls. But we had brilliant teachers and we got great exam results.

My parents didn't want us to grow up thinking we were the best. I think they saw an attitude in Foxrock which they didn't like and they wanted to make sure that their children stayed in touch with all sorts of people, not just the privileged set from the Southside.

I remember two brilliant teachers. One taught Latin and she was also the deputy headmistress. She was always quoting in Greek and Latin. She didn't see the girls just doing sewing or domestic science. She wanted us all to learn Classics. We were also able to do honours Maths, something which was not encouraged in girls' schools generally. There was also a great English teacher, who was exuberant and enthusiastic.

I was very good and boring at school. Because I was Margaret's sister and she was frequently in trouble I was often attacked because of her misdemeanours. My goody-good image hid my shyness.

Going to an all-girls school seemed natural. I send my

daughter now to a girls' convent in Ealing. Even though people laugh and say that I'm doing unto my child the sins that were done unto me, I think I have come out of it OK. Going to a single sex-school has made me a woman's woman. There are women who enter a room and look first for the men. I think because of my sisters and my school education I will always befriend a woman first. My first friends were women, my closest friends are now women and my loyalties are for women. A single-sex school helps to develop a bond or a sisterhood.

There is a strong bond between the girls in the family. We all talk on the phone every day and though we're very different, we're very close. Families seem more distant here. At home we spent a lot of time together. They are particularly gorgeous, intelligent women and I'm very proud of them. We are not just sisters, we are best friends.

We're all intelligent and achieved good results at school. I ended up with twenty-four academic points from my Leaving Certificate. We were in Dingle, County Kerry, on holidays when I got my results. I didn't know what to do. I had enough points to study medicine but I hated the sight of blood. I asked what were the other options and I was told law. I decided law it would be. I knew my father had always wanted to be a solicitor, and maybe that was part of the reason for my choice. It certainly wasn't an ambition that I had carried with me from early years. My father loved me doing law. I enjoyed studying most of it, though some parts were very boring. It was a narrow education and it should have been offered with an arts degree.

Despite the fact that we had brilliant teachers at St Anne's, the expectations for the girls from their parents were low. No matter how hard the teachers encouraged the pupils the parents didn't seem to follow it up. In my class just myself and another girl when to university. We both did Law!

I went to University College Dublin with my sister. She was nineteen and I was sixteen. Once again I had to go through the system with her. I'm sure in ways it must have affected me. I mean I was always the baby sister.

I was too young for university and I didn't really understand it. At the time I thought it was great and I was enjoying myself but if I went in now I would know what to do. I would meet everybody, join all the societies, do everything! Nobody really told me this was a chance to develop myself. I was like many others who ended up just using it to cram information into my head. My sister went and worked in the civil service for two years before studying for her degree and she really got a lot more out of it. She joined the debating society and was an active and dynamic debater. There should have been more career guidance when I finished school. I've done loads of films on education and I realise the importance of guiding people into the careers that will really suit them and make them happy.

I was incredibly shy during my college years. I meet people now who say that I appeared very confident. I hardly had any boyfriends; I was very reserved sexually with those I had. I was young, and emotionally very immature. I was completely unprepared for my growing sexuality. My mother had given me an Angela McNamara book to read, every Catholic girl's handbook. My mother meant well. She gave them to all of us when we were about twelve but of course we knew everything at that stage. I found out about sex from a girl called Barbara who lived down the road. I still remember being shocked by it. I thought it was the most awful thing and I ran off crying thinking it couldn't be possible. I wanted to tell my mother but I knew instinctively not to say anything. I just knew that I couldn't really discuss it with her. She is the best in the world but I knew it would embarrass her. Sex just was not talked about. I think that Irish parents have a lot of emotion to show but sex was definitely a 'no go' discussion topic. I never discussed it with my father, ever. Looking back I don't mind this but I think I would have liked to discuss things like relationships with him.

It must have been difficult for him with four beautiful daughters. When we were young he was affectionate but as we grew older he was hesitant showing us affection. I know from talking to friends of mine that they had similar experiences with their fathers. I don't think Irish men of his generation were encouraged to be comfortable with their daughters.

My parents encouraged me to follow my law studies with a solicitor's qualification. It seemed like a natural progression. I do think that some of the women went on to become solicitors not because they loved law but because they would meet a rich husband, although of course many really want to go on with law. I worked as a solicitor for two years and enjoyed it. There were moments when I felt truly bored but I never thought of doing anything else.

My husband however changed the direction of my life. I met him when I was eighteen and it was love at first sight. I knew when I saw him that I was going to marry him. I met him in a pub in Dublin, The Bailey. Tom walked in the door with a friend. I thought he looked nice. My friend Maria knew who he was. I went to the loo and he said something rude like 'Is it because you're so tall that you're so arrogant?' That was his chat-up line. He phoned me a few days later.

I found him very attractive physically and I liked his personality. He seemed unconventional. Because I was so straight he was everything I wasn't. Everybody told me different things about him. Eleven years older than me, people advised me that he wasn't the one for me. But I liked the way he encouraged me to question things. My mother married my father and he was eleven years older than her, and my sister has married a man eleven years older than her! I don't find the age gap a problem.

People in Dublin had bets on at our wedding, giving us six months. Everybody was very worried. I met Tom just that little bit too early but I have never regretted that meeting. I think it's probably better if you have the choice to wait until your mid-thirties to get married. By that stage you have had a chance to get a grip on your life and you can still have children. A lot of marriages break up because the two people are changing too much. Getting married so young was against what my parents wanted for me but I knew it was right for me.

I believe in marriage. I know all my friends who aren't married and are living together say that the commitments are just the same but I think they're different. I didn't live with Tom because of my background. My parents would have died! I knew that it would break every convention that they stood for. I wanted to marry him.

* * *

I'm probably a little religious. Raised a Catholic, I say my prayers and send my daughter to a convent school. I believe in God like an insurance policy. I just can't believe that there isn't anything. I find death very difficult to cope with. When my grandmother died, it surprised people that I appeared unmoved. I loved her. I used to meet her for a drink and introduce her to my friends. I was very close to her. I think I'm good at blocking out emotions that I can't deal with. I never show my emotions in public.

I find religion in Ireland deeply hypocritical. People believe that if you go to all the ceremonies you will be fine. Some of the horrible people I knew were people who used to go to mass. I know lots of people who don't attend a church who are far more Christian in the real sense. I dislike the Catholic Church's attitude to sexuality. The message in Ireland when I was growing up was that sex is a sin. The celibate nature of priesthood is unnatural although I have an uncle a priest, whom I like and respect and there are certainly many who are genuine in their vocation. I do feel that Ireland in ways has been sexually disturbed by some of the messages passed on from the Church. Maybe it has changed a lot since I've lived there. I hope so.

* * *

In 1983 I moved to England with my husband, who is a writer, because he wanted to work with Radio 4. When we came to London it was a new start and was exciting. We stayed for a fortnight in the Irish Club, and then moved out to share a flat with friends. It's quite lonely when you come from being a big fish in a small pond to a very large pond.

I remember in 1983 wondering if it would be possible to crack this society because it seemed so big and so bad. I liked the anonymity — nobody knew who we were; it was just Miriam and Tom; we could do what we liked without anybody spying on us. I was determined to make it here.

I moved to the fashion world, working with Cacharel. I convinced them I was capable of learning something about fashion. They hired me and flew me to Paris to scout for clothes. But I had decided by that time that I wanted to work in television.

I never knew anybody in television when I was growing up. In fact we were not allowed to watch it; we had to do our homework. But through Tom and his contacts I became very interested in it. I saw an ad in *The Guardian* and applied cold. I was called for interview. I had no television experience and you needed it for the job. I told them that I knew how the *Late Late Show* in Dublin worked. I hadn't appeared in the show but had been a member of the audience several times and was most interested in the studio operations. The post was for researcher for Eamonn Andrews' programme, *This is your Life*. They were hesitant about my lack of experience and didn't offer me the job at the first interview. I didn't hear from them for six months. But then I got a call and I resigned from the fashion world immediately.

The BBC team were quite apprehensive about me for the first few weeks but I loved it and ended up staying on that show for two years — they were the happiest years of my life. I was lucky in that Eamonn Andrews and myself clicked. He was great to work with. He treated me like 'a daughter,' and often joined me for lunch. We had great fun together and I travelled with the show to America. He said I was the best researcher he had ever had. And for me he was an Irish father figure at the helm of a really good show. My confidence grew and led me on to becoming a senior producer, presenter and reporter.

* * *

My education in Ireland has really helped me in Britain and I know that I have been able to avail of opportunities here because of it. I am driven by a will to do things that people don't expect me to do. In reporting jobs I have challenged the stereotype that I am not just a pretty face, that I am capable of doing serious work. There are still far more men in hard news and current affairs in TV and radio. Women are still perceived by many as the decorative presenters but it's slowly changing.

I have been incredibly lucky in the BBC. It's a bit like the civil service. If a department head likes your work you will be promoted. I work hard and would describe myself as a diplomatic worker. I am careful and courteous with people. But if people push me too far, I can flip and I can let it rip. I think people are so stunned because they don't expect it from me that they never do it again. Particularly men; they can be such cowards.

I admire Olivia O'Leary. She's an excellent political journalist and has been for many years. She is good, sharp and has a certain arrogance which makes her a formidable interviewer. But I don't admire many public figures. In this job you hear about all sides of politicians and celebrities, you investigate the failings which bring them tumbling from their pedestals! I think I'm more inspired by ordinary people who don't make the headlines but who cope with real life problems with courage and initiative.

I am currently working on an investigative film on Northern Ireland and I am amazed at how little I knew about the whole scenario there. I have met inspirational people there from both sides of the divide. Growing up in Dublin, in the Republic of Ireland, I realise how little the North of Ireland featured in our lives. We didn't discuss it. We didn't get involved. It seemed a million miles away and yet only sixty miles up the road. I don't have an answer to the troubles of Northern Ireland, but if people at least familiarised themselves with all the different strands of the situation that would be a start.

* * *

I would like to return home though I'm not sure my husband feels the same. I do feel the quality of life is better in Ireland. Ireland would be a much better home for our daughter. And besides, Dublin will always be home. I have great fun there.

Juggling motherhood and a full-time job is a real challenge. Any free time I have, I spend with my daughter. She is a great source of joy for me. I love being a mother. The bond between us sometimes nearly frightens me. I was leaving her to school recently, and another child pushed her. I could sense this tremendous indignation rising in me. I know I could kill to protect my child. The strength of my protective feeling for her surprised me.

One of the most important things to give a child is confidence

— a belief in their ability to do anything. One of the good things I find about London is that people are supportive. Although we Irish are a warm and friendly race, it's a tragedy that we feel we have to 'knock' each other. We're very good when people are down; we help them and reach out to them; but there is an underlying belief that nobody should be too big for their boots. Women are particularly pulled apart for stepping out of line. Women in Ireland need all the support they can get as they begin to step out of traditional roles.

I would like to have more children, maybe three of four more, but would not like to raise them in Britain. It's not a caring society. Maybe it's just London but people haven't got time to care in this city. I fell recently in a busy street and not one person stopped to help me up. It's only a small thing but that would never happen in Dublin. With the growing divisions in British society I often remark to my colleagues at work 'Well at least I don't have to stay here.'

Personal truths

Work hard.

Be loyal to your friends, family and the people you work with.

Never give up on your dreams.

Show your affection.

Cherry Smyth

Cherry Smyth is aged thirty-one and was reared in Portstewart in Northern Ireland. She is Lesbian Editor of **City Limits Magazine** *in London.*

After studying English and French at Trinity College, Dublin she emigrated to England in 1982 to study Film and TV at Middlesex Polytechnic. She has worked in Video Production, as a freelance researcher and as Film and Video Production Officer with Greater London Arts. Here she was responsible for assessing and funding scripts from independent film and video-makers.

She has produced and co-researched **Red Rosas**, *a 16mm documentary about the lives of older, radical, Jewish women. She has researched a book on the representation of women in cinema and contemporary debates and has done press and publicity work for The Women's Press and Virago. She is a guest film reviewer on BBC Radio 2's cinema programme.*

A tutor at the University of London's first Lesbian Cinema Course in 1990, she has arranged and presented a series of lesbian film and video screenings and discussion in independent cinemas.

Cherry has worked as a freelance journalist for a number of years. Specialising in film and TV culture she has had her work published in **Spare Rib, Feminist Review, Independent Media, Marxism Today** *and* **Rouge,** *a lesbian and gay socialist magazine. She has had short stories published in two anthologies of lesbian erotica,* **Serious Pleasure** *(1988) and* **More Serious Pleasure** *(1990).**

---

* Sheba Feminist Press.

She enjoys soul music, dancing, yoga, swimming, walking in the fresh air and travelling. Her pet resentments include gardening, people who interrupt others, gossip and lying.

I interviewed her in a small conservatory at the back of her North London home. Elegant, assertive and thoughtful, she is a writer who has grown through an Irish landscape.

CHERRY SMYTH

AT THE BEGINNING of 1990 I left a full-time job, which was quite pressurised, as an independent video producer for an arts body. It was enjoyable but my own creativity was suffering. Now I write film reviews and my own fiction. Even as a child I wrote poems and sort of twee little rhyming couplets. Then I studied English at Trinity College, Dublin. I loved English at school and reading aloud and my mum always read me poetry at night from the *Faber Book of Children's Verse*. When I studied at Trinity I decided that everything I wrote was derivative and I stopped writing. When I left college I went into film and video but now I've come back.

I always kept journals but what started me writing again was becoming a feminist and going to women's writing classes and realising that my experience was shared by other women and I could present it in a very potent way. I went to lesbian poetry readings and joined an Irish women's writing network. We went around Irish festivals, feminist book events, anything that wanted a cultural representation of Irish women. Our work ranged from the very lyrical, romantic, nostalgic images of Ireland to incest, male brutality, lesbian experiences, and bringing up children.

I was brought up in a loose tradition of performance. At Christmas we did these family get-togethers where everybody would have to do a piece like singing or reciting a poem. I've got tapes of when I was four years old reciting twenty verses of St John, Chapter 4. My great aunt who was an evangelical, a born-again Christian really encouraged self-expression as long as it was holy. My dad read an awful lot. If he used a word that you didn't understand he would really enjoy explaining it which made me interested in how words worked. I'm fascinated by them.

My aunt convinced me to become a born-again Christian when I was about eight or nine. That lasted for a few months and then I thought all my friends were going to hell and that even Mum and Dad would be down there and I'd be on my own with Auntie Vi. It would have been so boring.

I can remember going to revivalist meetings with her and asking the Lord Jesus to come into my heart with everyone waving hankies and crying 'I'm saved,' or 'I was a drunkard but not now.' It was extreme fundamentalism — all hellfire and damnation. If you had a guilty thought or didn't believe in the Prince of Peace you were going to be dammed; your coffin would explode at the end of the world. But I loved it, it was all so theatrical.

> *My childhood was full of light.*
> *Daz-white fluorescent gleaming on Formica surfaces.*
> *French toast for tea on Saturday nights.*
> (From *Coming Home*)

I'm the eldest of four and my aunt and grandfather lived with us on and off. There were four cousins who also lived with us for a while in Portstewart. It's on the coast of County Derry, a very beautiful place with a two mile stretch of strand. It hasn't really been affected by the troubles. It's mostly middle class and Protestant.

Growing up in Portstewart made me very responsive to nature. I loved the sea and I'd go for a walk every single day. It was very difficult when I moved to a city. I missed the sea incredibly and I still yearn for that now. If I feel depressed in London I want to get on the train to Brighton. I'm not used to being surrounded by a limited horizon. The restrictive nature of cities makes me search out the sea. I took up yoga when I went to Dublin. That was a way of relaxing without being in nature. I was completely spoilt in terms of beauty in my home town and it made me acutely aware of environmental issues. When I was seventeen, I wanted to campaign for lead-free petrol — everybody thought I was mad.

* * *

My father ran a drapery shop in a nearby town which he took over from his father. It started off as a shoe shop but it became a mini 'Jones Brothers.' It was destroyed by IRA incendiaries in the 1970s and my father had a severe mental breakdown. I decided that I was going to leave Northern Ireland because I felt nobody could see a way out of it. I certainly didn't want to have a family and kids growing up in an environment that I felt was strongly affected by death, through illness and the pressure on my father.

> *Kids running, petrol bombs,*
> *barricades and bin lids, cars on fire*
> *overturned on telly.*
>
> *On the news Dad's shop burning down.*
> *My mascara had run.*
>
> *Not everything was destroyed.*
> *That was worse.*
> *Salvaging charred dresses, wet shoes,*
> *scalded mannequins.*
> *Shawn chewed chewing gum.*
> *So did I.*
>
> *Daddy was quiet for a long time.*

(From *Maybe It was 1970*)

As a teenager, I was angry with the IRA, that they had picked on him. He wasn't a 'unionist bastard.' He was a councillor and had voted for equal opportunities in housing, employment and facilities. It would have been easier if I had felt he had deserved it. He really suffered. The shop was rebuilt but he could never pay his debts so he sold up and took early retirement. He was on medication for years after. He became cynical politically and I inherited that very quickly. He lost his political will. I think that's incredibly sad. It made me feel so powerless. I had no understanding of the IRA policy to debilitate Northern Ireland economically.

My paternal patriarchal respect was shattered. Dad, my role model was so shaken by the experience. And it was my mum who took over; she started to work. I felt this incredible loss and was suspicious of people in the street, thinking 'Did you do it? Did you do it because I'm Protestant? Are you pleased now?'

I was about seventeen when all this happened and it confirmed my decision to leave. I knew I wanted to get out of Northern Ireland but I didn't want to ditch Ireland altogether and I didn't want to go to England at that stage. From my high school you either went to Queen's University in Belfast or to Stranmillis Teacher Training College. There was little imaginative career advice. Though when the EEC came along we were suddenly given the choice to become bilingual secretaries in Brussels.

High school was a single-sex school and I was relieved to be away from the boys. It's a complex dynamic, competing with them and also wanting their approval. I loved wearing the uniform and I particularly loved the tie. The discipline at the school was petty. You had to tie your hair back, and you were only allowed to wear one ring and gold ear studs.

Looking back, it was tyrannical. My sister hated it, got suspended and left. But I, being the eldest and careful of approval, stayed on. I have written pieces about school and how I feel angry about the way we were taught history, through English history books, encoded so that we couldn't make an informed opinion about politics. Coupled with what was happening around us, politics seemed like a bad word. It was run by men and male politicians didn't know the answers. I rejected the whole thing. I remember Mum and Dad would turn up the news and I'd always leave the room, Consequently, I just lost out on a huge chunk of political development. I didn't know anything about Ireland and I didn't know anything about anywhere else. I thought news represented bad news, rows, family conflict. I had no respect for it. I felt politics equalled stupidity — mindless repetitions with no solutions. 'So I'm going to leave' — that was my attitude, not one thought of getting in there and fighting for it to be different.

* * *

It wasn't until I 'became a feminist' that I realised that women had an incredibly powerful role that had never been articulated and it gave me a way of seeing Ireland as a whole. The way you learn history and politics in Protestant schools in Northern Ireland is very divisive and it is all from a male, colonialist perspective. At school I remember clearly picking domestic science rather than chemistry because it would be more useful. I wanted to be able to choose a good saucepan. That was the way of becoming a good housewife in Northern Ireland. In my early teens, I believed that I would meet Mr Right; we'd have all the mod cons and each have our own cars and have two or three babies.

From very early on I was quite physical. With two younger brothers, I liked doing things that boys did. I hated missing out because I was a girl, so I played commandos, pirates, cowboys and Indians. I used to sit with my legs open and I was told to cross them in a ladylike manner. My mother is feminine and elegant. I always wanted to be like her but felt I would never achieve it.

My first lover was a hippy. He was my incarnation of rebellion. He'd meet me after school in this beaten-up old Volkswagen and we'd go off to this farm and have sex and all the time I was a prefect at the school. I had learnt about the facts of life from jokes, like 'Little girl sees her daddy in the bath and asks mummy, "What's that?" and she's told "That's Daddy's ship, which he puts into Mummy's harbour."' I remember a friend of mine, who was two years older than me and had older sisters, told me how babies were made. I was completely disgusted and didn't believe that Mum and Dad did it.

Nearly all the working class girls left school at fifteen and went to the technical school or had babies. The middle class girls went to Queen's and then some came back and taught at the school, or came back and lived locally. I decided to go to Trinity

133

College in Dublin to explore an Irish identity that I could claim. I didn't feel British and I didn't feel Irish.

My parents were proud that I went to Trinity. They really enjoyed the chance to go to Dublin. It was such a cultural capital, while the North was a cultural desert then. But I was disappointed. Most of the students from the South were living with their parents. I was on a grant and I had freedom. I was amazed at how ignorant people were about the North. I found people as prejudiced in Dublin as I did when I first came to England. Having a northern accent in Dublin was unusual and occasionally considered incomprehensible.

I thought I was pregnant at one point and I went to an abortion debate. I was pro-choice and was all set to go to England. A woman stood up and quoted the priest who said that a boy's soul was created at five weeks and the soul of a girl at seven weeks. I thought, 'This is ridiculous.' I wanted to challenge it but felt shy about doing it because I didn't have any political theory to fall back on, to contextualise a feminist argument.

* * *

I went to San Francisco when I was twenty-one. I bought loads of books and came into contact with gay pride and feminist groups. I thought this was amazing, so exciting. I knew I wanted to be part of it. Going back to Dublin I felt very alone and isolated.

At that point I thought I must go to England. It wasn't a conscious realisation that in England I could be a lesbian, more that I would be able to meet strong women, and be independent, have rights, and be taken seriously. From very early on I wanted to prove that I wasn't just a pretty face and that I wasn't going to be undermined by any man. This desire came from the way my mother has been restricted through her life. She is a very articulate, intelligent, creative woman and she's never been able to find an outlet for that. She has always been active in voluntary charity groups, but she undermines what she does. I felt that men didn't really respect women, that they liked to have a pretty woman on their arm and I knew that I wanted to be more than that.

Dublin I found stifling. It did open up the film world to me but it was also restricting, intellectually and politically. When I read James Joyce's *The Dubliners*, the image of paralysis and immobility rang true for me. I couldn't bear the provincialism or the hypocrisy. I just felt everybody was talking about getting out and yet there they were sitting in Bewley's drinking coffee.

* * *

Incessant boat people are we,
Forced from Larne to Stranraer,
Belfast to Liverpool,
Dun Laoghaire — Fishguard,
Limerick — Quebec,
Pale with separation
We drag slowly with suitcases and memories
To other lands.

(From *Coming Home*)

I arrived over in London with no place to live. I found myself at the end of the Piccadilly line at Cockfosters. I thought I was in this soap opera, all these tudorised shops and houses, and the English accent. I met this guy in a pub and I told him I had nowhere to live. He took me to see a mate of his who had a front room to rent. It was a half mile from the film and video college where I did a postgraduate course.

I started going to the cinema on my own, and travelling on the tube. I loved it. The different people, the fashion, everything. I was completely mesmerised. I took a course at the Haringey Women's Centre and had a lot of my ideas challenged in that first year. I felt accepted in London. I could be a vegetarian and people didn't think I was odd. It was a moving, challenging, uplifting, almost spiritual development.

I believe it is possible to have some sort of spirit existence. I believe in a sixth sense, which is translated through people you've loved and known, although I don't believe you go anywhere after you die; you decompose.

The Enniskillen bomb in 1988 really moved me, partly

because my grandmother came from Enniskillen and could have been in that crowd, although she died years ago. I felt incredibly guilty about being in England, about being in an occupying country, about not being in Ireland. I remember crying and going into work and nobody even knew about it.

Killing Enniskillen, killing.
Enniskillen will not linger
on front page news.
On front page news they're only Irish
and of course it happens there
all the time.

(From *Enniskillen*)

I went for a massage and the masseuse said she could 'feel' my grandmother. She asked me what my grandmother meant to me. I just burst into tears. I said 'I can't stop thinking about her since this thing in Enniskillen,' and she said 'Well, she's here and she's connecting with you.' I told my aunt, her sister, when I went home and she told me that my grandmother had died almost exactly at that time of year. It was a peaceful experience. I don't find it frightening.

If I lived in Ireland I'd be much more aware of my spirituality. I'd follow my instinct and I'd be more responsive to hidden things in other people. You've time to notice these sorts of things when you're in a rural environment and in an environment which people respect. I miss the rituals of going to church or chapel. I love going to hear classical music recitals and singing. I feel safe in a church. I miss that time for meditation. I feel excluded from these processes as a lesbian and as an agnostic.

The most moving spiritual thing I've been involved in was a memorial service for people who have died from AIDS. It was in St James's, in Piccadilly. There were Protestant and Catholic hymns, Hindu readings, Buddhist prayers, Jewish texts, arias and every denomination and all age groups were there. If this sort of thing was available for me, I would be involved in it, something inter-denominational which does not preach 'one faith is the only faith.'

When I was young I made pacts with God and he didn't keep them. Growing up in Northern Ireland I thought God can't exist if this sort of thing goes on. I don't think this is a religious war; it's not as simple as that. I felt completely disillusioned with Christianity. I also must have felt that the people around me who were Christians were bigots and hypocrites. I think the Church's attitude to women made me feel guilty about my body and having intercourse. Though I shook a lot of that off when I decided to be lesbian.

The very idea of getting one man to say 'I now pronounce you man and wife,' and then having to go to another one if you want to divorce is demeaning. The whole legal system puts women down and the Church compounds that. It's detrimental to woman's freedom.

* * *

Coming to England, I really immersed myself in feminism. I was involved in the Greenham Common peace demo, in non-violent direct action, and in a rape support group. I read a lot about male violence. For me it was connected with violence at home in Northern Ireland. It was quite a simplistic analysis — men were military and women were not.

I developed strong friendships with women and felt I didn't have to compete with them, I didn't have to be anything I couldn't be. I began to know women who were separatist. At this point I was living in a mixed house and working at a mixed community video workshop. The politics of separatism made me think 'I have given so much time and energy to men in my life that I am not going to do it anymore.' I realised that I had always been involved with men who were very effeminate, and I was like their mother! It just seemed like a waste of energy and I started to think 'If she was a man I'd want to sleep with her,' and then my desires started changing. It's not that I was 'born' a lesbian. It's been much more about the choices I've made in my life. I don't know if I'm going to decide that I'd like to live with a man in ten years time and have babies. I might! But at this point in my life, women's perspectives on the world are important to me and my desire is motivated by being a lesbian.

I became fed up with the separatist argument, though it did encourage a huge blossoming of my own creativity. I ran women-only video courses and attended feminist writing classes, and learnt to paint. But with the separatist movement I felt I shouldn't talk to my father and brothers. I couldn't live in a mixed house. I felt uncomfortable with that; it was unforgiving and inhumane.

I do understand separatism, in the same way that I support black sections of the Labour party wanting to go off on their own, to recover their strength — but 'bring it back,' that's what I believe. I support coming back, whether it's to do with race, gender or sexuality.

I was very angry then. Angry with all men, all politicians, the IRA; they were all in the one basket. I felt exhausted with anger. More recently I've felt less interested in being rigidly separatist. I'm not going to be told by another feminist that I can't wear lipstick or can't flirt with someone or wear a skirt. I don't have to have my sexuality defined by a certain camp. I also campaign alongside gay men who have given me huge support and friendship, especially around Clause 28 and censorship issues.

Living in England has given me the space to work out these ideologies. Portstewart would definitely have been far too claustrophobic, far too confining, and defining. I find it hard to go back. I regress to being an eighteen year old heterosexual though my parents know that I am a lesbian. They have always encouraged me to be honest and confide in them. They were incredible when I told them. 'Well,' they said, 'you have always given us great joy and we accept what makes you happy.'

If I went back to Dublin, I might get a lot out of it. But the moral attitude would make me feel guilty and apologetic for who I am. There are a lot of Irish lesbians living in Britain because they feel that they have not the freedom to be visible in Ireland.

* * *

Cherry Smyth and Friend, Nasreen

Photograph: Jean Fraser

I've learnt a lot about my own racism living in Britain. I'm really glad that England has given me that opportunity. There are great alliances being made here among black women and Irish women against racism and under-representation.

> *How can I ring Ireland*
> *not sounding happy, gregarious, fulfilled?*
> *Must never slip into loneliness,*
> *certainly never cry.*

(From *Night Creams*)

When I first came to England I didn't want to meet Irish people. I just wanted to get away from it, not to have to justify my position on Northern Ireland, not to have to think about it. Then slowly I began to crave it, to miss it and that's when I joined the Irish writing group. There are a lot of things about Ireland I can't write about because they are painful, like growing up in Northern Ireland — a guy I was at primary school with was shot, my father's business and health destroyed, the whole atmosphere of militarism was very oppressive.

> *They won't forget.*
> *And they'll send more boys*
> *with armoured cars and armoured minds*
> *to pump through narrow country lanes,*
> *camouflaged with Tyrone fields and hedges.*
> *They won't forget what they were taught*
> *about the thick Paddy,*
> *the mindless people*
> *killing each other.*
> *They'll go on mopping up the mess they leave.*

(From *Enniskillen*)

I support taking the troops out of Northern Ireland. I have visions of doing it surreptitiously. I do think that you would need a UN peace keeping force, something more neutral, to go in during the interim period. But the sectarianism and terrorism on both sides are very deep. It's not simply about taking out the troops. It's about equality for women and Catholics. It's about better housing conditions, better jobs for everyone so that there isn't this whole hierarchical resentment between people. The RUC should be disbanded and reconstructed so that a quota of Catholics and Protestants could be recruited. At the moment, it is a force tainted by corruption and not accepted by the community.

I have been strongly influenced by my father's original interest in politics. My lesbianism is political. I was chair of the Women's Film and TV Network, promoting women in the media, pushing for more programming and funds for women's issues. I was also involved in a group called Campaign for Press and Broadcasting Freedom which was anti-censorship. In my writing and readings I try to be out, open and honest.

I have taken risks both in my writing and teaching around lesbian representation. I believe strongly that women could have less repressed attitudes to their bodies and their sexual desires if there were more spaces to present positive images and texts. I have tried to open up dialogues around taboo subjects and have written about sex in explicit detail in stories which have been dubbed 'lesbian erotica' by some and 'dirty porn' by others. It is essential that women do not naïvely follow censorship demands 'to protect' women from explicit material as it may further restrict women's access to information, expression and explorations around their own sexuality. I have also done work around the representation of women and AIDS and believe that frank discussions of sexual activities are vital to counter the risk of infection, illness and untimely death.

* * *

Britain at the moment has regressed in terms of personal freedom. There's a real ethos of white middle class men running the country for money power. It has certainly affected the Irish community here. We've never been taken seriously as an ethnic minority, even though we are the biggest one in the country. Progressive radical ideas are being put down and it's affecting artists, writers and political groups, the voluntary sector, everything. But at the same time I am better off than if I was in

Ireland. I have more access to resources and support, although I have had to sacrifice many elements of my culture and personality in England and feel a deep sense of loss of Ireland. I miss aspects of the language, humour and self-deprecating wit. I also have great respect for those who stay on there and challenge the *status quo*, and also those who choose to return with the knowledge, self-confidence and skills they have gained abroad.

I don't feel as if I have left Ireland. I've emigrated but haven't really said Goodbye. So I find it hard to think that I will live here for the rest of my life. There is a sense of homelessness. I'm certainly not rooted in this country. That whole sense of place is very important to Irish people, like where you are from and the name of your family and the name of your little area. Here it's much more disparate and fragmented.

I find it hard to think of the future. I was recently discussing this with a friend of mine who also grew up in Northern Ireland, and we both have a feeling of insecurity, of not knowing what is going to happen in the next three years. It's an inherent level of fear. Also being anti-nuclear, I was terrified by the bomb as a teenager, and now of course the earth itself is at risk ecologically.

I know I want to be a writer, and write film scripts with good positive women in them. I want to continue writing radio plays. I want to go on being seen and heard and expressing myself.

I'd love to have kids, but it's so much more premeditated when you're a lesbian. It's not going to happen on a casual night. Sometimes I wish I'd done it when I was eighteen. I'd love to experience it, but I wonder is it indulgent? I think perhaps I should foster or adopt. Then I think I do want to have children, to procreate. I've decided that my novel will be my baby. I try and put my energy into my writing when I'm broody.

> *Memories of Ireland are ice*
> *And sunlight which falls*
> *Down an escalator,*
> *Always in the same place*
> *Yet never still.*

(From *Coming Home*)

142

Personal truths

(Both of these I got from my parents; they still ring true for me.)

If at first you don't succeed, try, try and try again.

If you can't say something nice about somebody, say nothing.